Every Season

embracing a *forever* kind of *purpose*

Stonecroft
where she is ✢ as she is

pp. 92-93 Excerpt from Stories for a Faithful Heart: Over One Hundred Treasures to Touch Your Soul by Alice Gray, copyright © 1999 by Multnomah Publishers, Inc. Used by permission of WaterBrook Multnomah, an imprint of the Crown Publishing Group, a division of Penguin Random House LLC. All rights reserved. Any third party use of this material, outside of this publication, is prohibited. Interested parties must apply directly to Penguin Random House LLC for permission.

pp. 46-47 Taken from Living Beyond the Limits: A Life in Sync with God by Franklin Graham copyright © 1998 by Franklin Graham. Used by permission of Thomas Nelson. www.thomasnelson.com

Unless otherwise indicated, all Scripture quotations are taken from the Holy Bible, New Living Translation, copyright © 1996, 2004, 2015 by Tyndale House Foundation. Used by permission of Tyndale House Publishers, Inc., Carol Stream, Illinois 60188. All rights reserved.

Scripture quotations marked (MSG) are taken from THE MESSAGE, copyright © 1993, 1994, 1995, 1996, 2000, 2001, 2002 by Eugene H. Peterson. Used by permission of NavPress. All rights reserved. Represented by Tyndale House Publishers, Inc.

Scripture quotations marked (ESV) are from The Holy Bible, English Standard Version®, copyright © 2001 by Crossway Bibles, a publishing ministry of Good News Publishers. Used by permission. All rights reserved.

Scripture quotations marked (NIV) are taken from the Holy Bible, New International Version®, NIV®. Copyright © 1973, 1978, 1984, 2011 by Biblica, Inc.™ Used by permission of Zondervan. All rights reserved worldwide. www.zondervan.com The "NIV" and "New International Version" are trademarks registered in the United States Patent and Trademark Office by Biblica, Inc.™

Designed and Typeset by Serena Lilli Jeanne

Written by Janice Mayo Mathers

ISBN: 978-0-9908500-9-0

Produced and Distributed by:

Stonecroft
10561 Barkley, Suite 500
Overland Park, KS 66212

800.525.8627 / connections@stonecroft.org

stonecroft.org

© 2018, Stonecroft, Inc. All right reserved. The right to use any portion of this book may be secured by written permission. The views, opinion, and positions expressed in this book are those of the author and do not necessarily reflect the views, opinions, or positions of Stonecroft.

Contents

welcome to stonecroft bible studies — 5

tips for using this study — 6

introduction — 9

chapter 1
His Handiwork — 15

chapter 2
Glorify & Worship God — 29

chapter 3
Salt & Light — 45

chapter 4
Trust God — 59

chapter 5
Be His Image-Bearer — 73

chapter 6
Bear Fruit — 87

conclusion
Final Thoughts — 99

God's pursuing love — 105

notes	109
works cited	110
who is Stonecroft?	113
resources	115
about the author	117

Acknowledgments

We acknowledge and thank Janice Mayo Mathers for her dedication in serving the Lord through Stonecroft. Speaker, author, and member of Stonecroft's National Board of Directors, Jan is the author of *Ephesians: Made Complete in Christ*. We appreciate her love for God's Word and her love for people who need Him.

Special thanks go to the team who prayed for Jan, and those who edited, designed, and offered their creative input to make Stonecroft Bible Studies accessible to all.

– Stonecroft

In memory of
Leona Dyksterhuis Selee

Her passions were loving Jesus and sharing her faith with other people. Leona was a true friend of Stonecroft, a student of the Bible, and a woman who delighted in celebrating God's creation. Our prayer is that those who use this Bible study will enjoy it in the company of others and through it discover their own purpose for glorifying God in every season.

– Stonecroft

Welcome to Stonecroft Bible Studies!

It doesn't matter where you've been, what you've done, or what has happened to you – God wants to be in relationship with you. And one place He tells you about Himself is in His Word: the Bible. Whether the Bible is familiar or new to you, its contents will transform your life and bring answers to your biggest questions.

Gather with people in your communities – women, men, couples, young and old alike – and consider the truth that God created you for purpose, His purpose. Reflect on the faithfulness of God to bring about His good pleasure in every season of your lives.

Each chapter of *Every Season* includes discussion questions to stimulate meaningful conversation, specific Scriptures to investigate, and time for prayer to connect with God and each other.

Discover more of God and His ways through this small-group exploration of the Bible.

Tips for Using This Study

Every Season includes several features to make it easy and helpful for you:

- The page numbers given after every Bible reference are keyed to the page numbers in the Abundant Life Bible. This paperback Bible uses the New Living Translation, a translation in straightforward, up-to-date language. We encourage you to obtain a copy through your group leader or at stonecroft.org/store.

- Each chapter includes Bible stories retold in a way that encourages readers to feel they are participants in the scenes. The chapters also end with a section called "Reflect and Share." Journal pages are available for thoughts that come to you during your group or individual study times, as well as prayer requests.

- Please make this book and study your own. We encourage you to use it and mark it in any way that helps you grow in your relationship with God.

If you find this study helpful, you may want to explore additional resources from Stonecroft. Please look at Stonecroft "Resources" in the back of the book (Page 115), or online at stonecroft.org/store.

Introduction

When I was a parent of preschoolers, life felt constantly chaotic. Survival sometimes seemed the only goal. Living out my God-designed purpose rarely entered my mind. For me, purpose came in sizes 2 and 4 super-hero shirts running through the house with Superman capes made from dish towels pinned to their backs. Their purpose was clear – save the world from evil, though from my perspective their techniques looked more like demolition and destruction! But saving the world can be messy business. Just ask God!

One Friday morning defined this season of my life. Company was coming that night so my to-do list grew longer than usual. I had the living room polished and vacuumed and moved on to the guest bedroom. As I got started there, I heard whispered giggles coming from the living room. Never a good thing.

I peeked around the corner and gasped in horror. Four-year-old Tyler was running around the room shaking a large bottle of silver glitter. Showers of the stuff settled onto every piece of furniture. Two-year-old Landon danced behind him, delighted by the cascading sparkles.

Banishing the boys to their room to play with Legos, I started over in the living room. When I got to the guest bedroom again, I found the boys had beaten me to it. "Look, Mommy! We're helping!" Tyler proudly held up the economy-size can of Comet cleanser he'd been sprinkling over everything in the room.

"Helping!" Landon echoed as he smoothed the bluish-white grit into a new bedspread. Can you see why the big question of my life's purpose was far from my mind during this season? Still, this episode was not complete.

The last room to be cleaned was our master bedroom which we recently carpeted – my favorite room in the house. When I opened the door to get started, my eyes immediately fell on a large black stain in the middle of the room. Beside it lay an empty bottle of permanent black ink. I collapsed in a heap of tears, utterly devastated.

A phone call to my mom did little to soothe. "Honey, I know it seems as if this season of your life will last forever," she said. "But believe me, a blink of your eyes and it will be gone. You have to find a way to cherish this season."

Cherish? This season? Really? Could that seriously be the advice she offered? I sat for a while in silence. I had no response.

Our company arrived and politely ignored the hints of chaos lurking in the corners. The next day dawned shiny new as did the day after that and the day after that. Our boys progressed from preschoolers to teenagers to young adults, and somehow managed to become contributing members of society. And one day I realized my mother had been right.

First, in the blink of my eye this season passed – as have all the other seasons of my life.

And second, discovering a way to cherish each season – both the good and bad – provides help to find the key to fulfilling my purpose in life.

Emily P. Freeman, author of *A Million Little Ways*, tells of a conversation she had with a fellow passenger on a plane. When he asked her what her life motto was, she took time to answer, to give a thoughtful response. After a few moments she said, "I want to live my life less like a list and more like a lyric."[1]

What a great life motto! The truth is, our lives, when lived in harmony with God's design, when learning to read His sheets of music, will be lyrical. God moments, notable encounters, holy exchanges, significant interactions, and the like, will overshadow the daily grind of to-do lists that clutter our minds and can crowd out our sense of purpose.

Lists are important – no argument there. I live by sticky notes! But lists have a subtle way of elbowing out the sense of purpose God built into us. We do not exist on this Earth just to do laundry, to build that next presentation, or make the next promotion. We aren't even in this world to find the cure for cancer, educate children, or renovate the living room. God's purpose, implanted within each human being long before conception, far exceeds any human-conceived purpose.

As we age, maintaining a sense of purpose sometimes becomes more challenging. A subtle change comes over our daily lists, making them feel less purposeful: babysitting grandkids vs. raising kids, lending a hand vs. making a difference, doctor's appointments vs. vital meetings, the narrowness of caregiving vs. the wideness of building a career and, ultimately, marking time vs. making time count. Do you ever feel this way?

Is it possible to maintain an ongoing, motivating sense of purpose as we age? Is it possible to continue to live purposeful lives as our hair grays, our wrinkles deepen, and as a culture that places great value on youth and beauty fades us to the background?

The answer: A resounding YES! Aging offers tremendous advantages. The significant gift that accompanies the steady accumulation of years creates a truer life perspective. This deepening perspective can enhance our sense of purpose, especially when we understand God's definition of purpose. The great joys and deep sorrows we've experienced, the answers we've discovered and questions we've come to terms with – equip and fuel us for a rich and fruitful season of life. The secret lies in keeping our hearts open and eager, our hands willing and accepting of God's purpose, in every season and circumstance.

Discovering this purpose and living it out in every season and circumstance of life is what this Stonecroft Bible Study unfolds for you. We'll learn about God's purpose for us, as well as explore how to best sense and fulfill it as we travel each season of life.

Thank you for joining this study. Whatever season you find yourself in today, this focused time in God's Word offers you help to live each day with His powerful purpose. This time will help you see the opportunity to cherish each season on your life journey.

Reflect and Share

What purposes do you find in your life today?
Where has God placed you, and who are you serving?

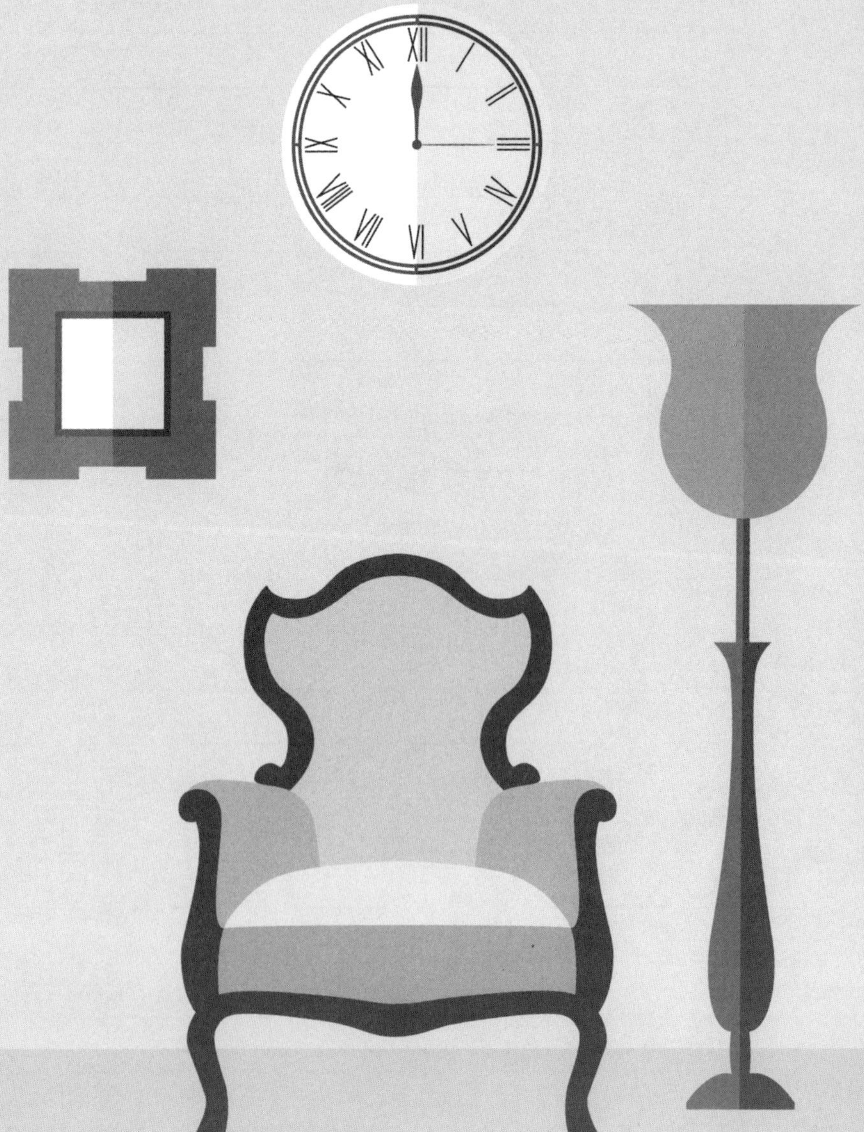

chapter 1

His Handiwork

"For we are God's handiwork, created in Christ Jesus to do good works, which God prepared in advance for us to do."

– Ephesians 2:10, NIV

It didn't take long for Ed to move to Michigan where Joy lived. He had prayed a long time about meeting the right girl and that special day with her on the coast seemed to be the start of something big!

Joy's life was filled with, well, joy! She waited to find the best man for her future – and Ed proved that this wait was well worth it! One year later these two late-20-somethings were married.

Five years into their marriage, their life didn't seem to be taking the shape they expected. Lots of school and work, but no pregnancy. Infertility treatments came and went. And the roller coaster of emotions took a toll. Hopes arose only to be dashed with disappointing news again and again.

> Do you have expectations that never quite seem to be fulfilled? What do you do with unmet expectations?

For Joy, one of those roller-coaster moments occurred on a Saturday morning. She was certain she was finally pregnant. Her hope rising, she took a pregnancy test. Once more the results were negative. At that moment, the phone rang. A friendly and empathetic voice on the other end provided comfort and then the conversation transitioned to a new topic, an unexpected topic – adoption.

"Joy, we just found out that a young friend of ours is pregnant who needs an adoptive couple." *Adoption? That is not on my radar,* Joy thought. She took a deep breath and said she would need to talk with Ed.

Then, the adoption fell through. Two weeks before the baby was born, the mother changed her mind.

Anger joined disappointment. Anger toward God. The questions mounted. "How could Ed be one of six children and I be one of five and we are not given the privilege of childbirth?" "How could You get our hopes up with a birth mother only to have them dashed?" Her pointed honesty with God continued, "You are not giving us the desire of our heart. Father, you tell us to be 'fruitful and multiply'" ... on and on the heart-wrenching prayers continued.

> Have you experienced repeated disappointment?
> Do you ever get so honest with God it comes out
> as anger? How do you think God responds?

For Joy, it took months and months of agonizing prayer to realize something important – even vital. Her prayers were trying to get God in on her plan rather than asking for God to reveal His plan for her. This was Joy's higher perspective and understanding for this season.

Yielding to God's plan takes enormous surrender, but Joy and Ed discovered God's faithfulness. Today, after two successful adoptions, Joy and Ed are empty nesters serving the Lord abroad working with military men and women, many of them struggling with dating, marriage, infertility, parenting, loss, and unfulfilled expectations.

When has this happened to you? You fight to realize your expectations only to have them redirected. Suddenly you are in a place you never intended or expected. Sometimes it's as simple as unexpected company and sometimes it's a life-altering experience or even tragedy. No matter how carefully we draw the map for our lives, or how much thought we put into the route we create, the road invariably takes us to unknown territory.

God's map (or plan) is unalterable and indestructible. Regardless of how random life might appear, or how purposeless it seems during some seasons, God's individual map for each one of us is sure and true. The route named *My Plan* leads all the way to the very last inch of our journey. Not one mile is pointless, not one second of Earth time lacks purpose when we are in harmony with Him. In fact, He even uses those times we are not on key for His plans.

> To form an understanding of just what our purpose is, we need to go back to the very beginning. Read Genesis 1:1-25 (Page 3). What does this passage tell us about God?

In the beginning God created.... Our very first glimpse into God's character reveals His creativity. These first 25 verses of Genesis 1 depict the staggering scope of God's creativity. And that's just an overview. Missing are mentions of the wonder of gravity, the capacity of the circulatory system, the complexity of the brain, the cycle of the seasons, and the marvel of variety in all living species. We don't even know yet all the beings God created! Humans know of about 2 million species on Earth. Eighteen thousand new species were discovered in 2016 alone! These 25 brief verses describe things humans tried to explain and understand for thousands of years.

In the next two verses, we read one of the most humbling, awe-inducing passages in all the Bible – a passage to which we don't give nearly enough thought. Read Genesis 1:26-27 (Page 3). What phrase is mentioned twice?

In His image! God – the creator of the Universe and everything in it – made you and me and the person sitting next to you, and your neighbor, and the person in front of you at the grocery store, and the crazy driver tailgating you – in His image! Read these two verses again slowly; take a few minutes to contemplate the personal implications of this passage. What thoughts come to your mind?

Look, if we are indeed created in God's image, then we can develop His character traits. His creativity can be expressed through us. His love, compassion, and patience can all be shown within and through us. This is why we are often called His "image-bearers."

But where God's nature has no limitations, our human nature does. We are not God, nor can we become a god as some spiritual belief systems teach. We cannot think or act our way into the perfection of God. When sin (going against God and His ways) entered the world through Adam and Eve (Genesis 2:25-3:6, Page 4), the image of God within us became distorted and the relationship between God and humanity was broken.

The Bible shows us that God, who made our hearts and understands how we think (Psalm 33:15, Page 427), has deep love and compassion for us and a great desire for relationship with us. So, He made a way, the one way, to address the sin that separates us from Him and mars the reflection of His image in us. Ephesians 2:10 (ESV) reads, "For we are his workmanship, created in Christ Jesus for good works, which God prepared beforehand, that we should walk in them."

What does it say we are to do?

Notice it does not say we are His artwork, His project, or His attempt. We are God's workmanship. We – you – are made "created in Christ Jesus"! Because of Jesus' willingness to die in our place, to pay the price for our rebellion against God, we have, today, new life! New life with meaning: "to do the good things he planned for us" (NLT). Astounding!

In Genesis, we learned we are created in God's image. Ephesians 2:10 affirms we are created in Jesus Christ!

Read 2 Corinthians 5:15-18 (Page 884).

Our sinful nature marred our original image, but God looked at the damage and brings restoration to those who believe in Him. He sent His only Son, Jesus Christ, to live on this Earth, fully human and fully God, to endure all the same sorrows, trials, and temptations we face, yet without giving in to sin's pull. Jesus Christ lived out God's purpose without faltering, even as He was put to death – not for His sins but for ours. Then He came back to life three days later. Through His life, death, and resurrection, Jesus made the following possible:

1. experiencing a reconciled relationship with God
2. resisting the pull of sin, through His Holy Spirit within us
3. living an abundant life now and an eternal life with God after our earthly life ends.

> The NLT version of Ephesians 2:10 (Page 896) puts it this way: "created anew in Jesus Christ." Through the death and resurrection of Jesus Christ, God made our restoration possible. How does 2 Corinthians 3:18 (Page 883) relate to this?

God's Spirit within us provides us the motivation and power to become more and more like Him. We are in the process of being conformed to the image of His Son. This transformation occurs as we behold the glory of the Lord. We behold His glory and find it beautiful because God has shone in our hearts to give the light of the knowledge of the glory of God in the face of Jesus Christ (2 Corinthians 4:6, Page 884). How exciting and encouraging it is to know that God who began this good work in us will continue His work until it is finally finished on the day that Christ Jesus returns (Philippians 1:6, Page 899).

Created to do good things. Now there's a broad topic for you! Wouldn't it be nice if in God's sovereignty He would make those words read differently for each of us? Created to be a good chef, created to be a good teacher, created to feed the hungry, adopt orphans. The phrase "good things" seems so general. It could apply to any career field, activity, mission, and stage of life. It applies to a time of illness, grief, celebration, joy – any season of life. His significance for us in this life is not so much about our career choice or the title we hold. It's not about the position we hold, but about the posture we possess because we are created in God's image. It's not about what we become professionally, but who we are spiritually. As the Apostle Paul put it, "you are a letter from Christ showing the result of our ministry among you. This 'letter' is written not with pen and ink, but with the Spirit of the living God. It is carved not on tablets of stone, but on human hearts" (2 Corinthians 3:3, Page 883).

> When people look at you, what do they see? Who do they see?
>
>
> What adjustments are you prepared to make to better reflect the image of God?

Perhaps you're currently in a season of life that seems lacking in significance. You go through the motions without any real sense of mattering to anyone. Let's look at the life of Anna, a Bible character. Though we know little about her, we can learn much from her.

> Read Luke 2:36-40 (Page 781).

Here's what we learn about Anna:
- She was a prophetess
- She was old – 84 years!
- She had been a widow for decades
- She was pious, spending much of her time in the temple
- She was granted special insight from God about Jesus' identity
- She understood God's plan for a Savior
- She unashamedly shared the Good News she knew

In these few verses, we glimpse an outline of Anna's life. God wanted us to know about her – at least about this moment in her life. We don't see the day after day after day of her time spent in the temple. We don't see the repeated path she wore to and from the temple. We are left to wonder if she was cared for by any children. Did the priests welcome her at the temple or deride her daily presence? Did others know her and extend friendliness, or did they roll their eyes at her persistent devotion?

Anna had been married and we can imagine she expected her life map to lead to a family, growing old with her husband, grandchildren, and retirement. Her marriage ended at her husband's death after just seven years. Perhaps you can relate to the devastation she probably suffered.

At some point, it appears, she fought any continued bitterness and despair. Anna chose to fix her eyes on God. She resolutely kept putting one foot in front of the other on the path God spread before her.

Take a few steps in Anna's sandals. When her husband died, she eventually focused on the one thing she knew she could do in the face of her new reality – pray. And that's what she did *for the rest of her life*.

Who and what do you think she prayed for all those years? For whom did she fast?

She was a woman just like us, but she kept her hands open before God and every day released her cherished dreams into His care. He, in turn, opened her eyes to God's plan for her that would be recorded in Luke for generations to read: prayer. There in the temple day after day, she had a first-row seat to the life-dramas taking place around her – sidetracked lives, broken hearts – and she prayed. As she prayed she kept her hope fixed on God's promise of a Messiah, a King to save the people. She possibly prayed for His arrival daily and watched in confidence. One morning she noticed a young couple enter the temple. They carried an infant and Anna approached for a closer look.

> Read again Luke 2:38 (Page 781).

From waiting to proclaiming! *Our Savior has arrived!* He is here! Anna became an eyewitness to and a proclaimer of the promise of God. She saw the Messiah with her own eyes. The most remarkable part of this story is that Anna was not deceived by the fact her Savior arrived in the shocking form of a baby instead of the king her people were expecting. She knew this baby was the Savior for whom her people were waiting. She began right then and there to spread the news to everyone within earshot.

Are you wondering if God has a tangible purpose for you, right now, in this season, at your age? Are circumstances making you feel sidelined, maybe even invisible? Know this: you're not a random piece of creation without a specific purpose. You're not one of 8 billion others just like you. You're not even one of eight others just like you. You are a one-of-a-kind creation God carefully designed. He created you to be in relationship with Him and to serve as His ambassador – His representative – to your area of the world. His identity is stamped on your heart. His road map is designed for you with His purpose clearly marked. With every person you talk to, with every thought you think, every obligation you fulfill, every errand you run, *be God's ambassador.*

Read 2 Corinthians 5:20 (Page 884).

According to this verse, what does it mean to be an ambassador?

Reflect and Share

Write the names of three people who especially need to see Christ represented through you. Pray for these three every day this week.

Closing Prayer

Father, help me every single morning to put on my new nature, created to be like You – truly righteous and holy. Keep reminding me that my old self has been crucified with Christ. It is no longer me living in my body but Christ living in me, so help me trust in Your Son who loved me and gave Himself up for me. Let me always be a light to the world, like a city on a hilltop that cannot be hidden. Let my words and actions shine for all to see, so that everyone will praise You. Amen. (Ephesians 4:24, Page 897; Galatians 2:20, Page, 891; Matthew 5:14, 16, Page 736.)

In the next session, we'll look more closely at God's purpose for His creation to gain a better understanding of how we can accomplish this purpose.

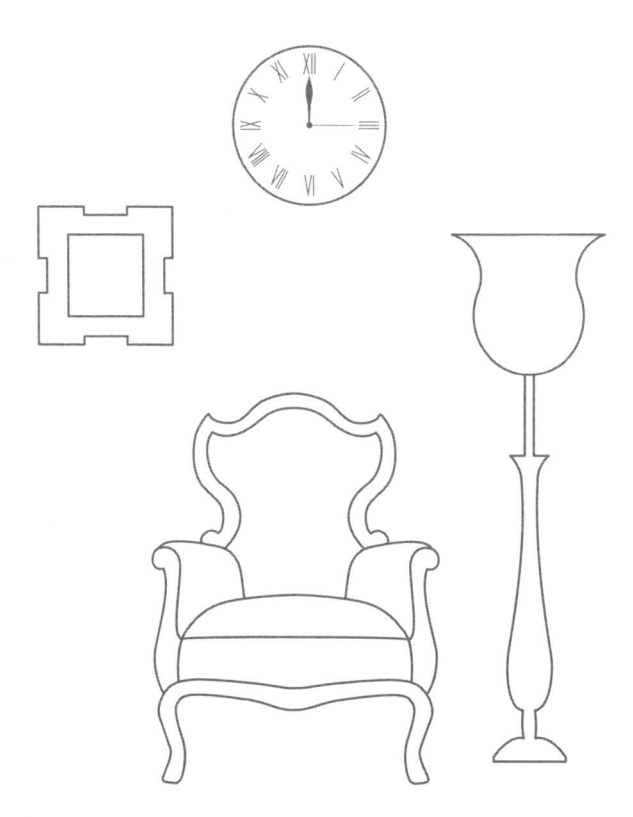

12
1
2
3
4
5
6
7
8
9
10
11

chapter 2

Glorify & Worship God

"So whether you eat or drink, or whatever you do, do it all for the glory of God."

– 1 Corinthians 10:31 (Page 876)

Let's read together Luke 10:38-42 (Page 793):

"As Jesus and the disciples continued on their way to Jerusalem, they came to a certain village where a woman named Martha welcomed him into her home. Her sister, Mary, sat at the Lord's feet, listening to what he taught. But Martha was distracted by the big dinner she was preparing. She came to Jesus and said, 'Lord, doesn't it seem unfair to you that my sister just sits here while I do all the work? Tell her to come and help me.' But the Lord said to her, 'My dear Martha, you are worried and upset over all these details! There is only one thing worth being concerned about. Mary has discovered it, and it will not be taken away from her.'"

When someone important to you plans to have dinner at your house, how do you react? Here's how I imagine Martha that day:

> Martha was beside herself with excitement. Her favorite person in the whole world had just shown up on her doorstep! Thrilled beyond words, she welcomed him with open arms. She led him into the living room where he could relax in comfort. The day was warm and he'd walked quite a distance, so she brought him a cold drink before hurrying off to the kitchen, her mind whirling with ideas for the delicious meal she would fix for him. She wanted him to know how much he meant to her, how much she appreciated all he was doing.
>
> As she flew around the kitchen, chopping, stirring, kneading, she listened to the sounds of easy conversation and laughter coming from the living room. *Good!* she thought. *Mary's entertaining him. She's so great at that.* Her heart bubbled with joy at this unexpected visit. She wanted to do everything she could to make it perfect.
>
> She continued her work. The kitchen heated up as the vegetables boiled and the bread baked. She swiped at her damp forehead

and reached to bring plates down from the cupboard. *Was Mary ever going to quit talking and come help her? Didn't she realize she'd like to be visiting with Jesus, too – but then who'd fix dinner?*

Her pleasure in serving her friend came under attack by resentment and self-pity.

The story is just five verses long. Let's take a closer look at the story.

> Read again Luke 10:38-42 (Page 793).
>
> What is the first thing you learn about Martha?
>
>
>
>
> Her first action is right on target, isn't it? She welcomed Jesus into her home. What's the second thing Martha does?

Oops! In this crazy-busy world it's easy to become distracted, isn't it? We start off well; our joy is intact, our energy is high, our focus is right on. Then something distracts us. It can be as insignificant as a rude driver. The distraction kidnaps our thoughts and holds them ransom until we relinquish our focus on what is good and then we wallow in what isn't. It's all downhill from there.

When we set our hearts upon God, and He transforms our minds from the earthly to the eternal, we begin to understand worship as more than something we do – sing, pray, praise – and more about how we live.

> Romans 11:33-36 (Page 866):

"Oh, how great are God's riches and wisdom and knowledge!

How impossible it is for us to understand his decisions and his ways!

"For who can know the LORD's thoughts?

Who knows enough to give him advice?

"And who has given him so much

that he needs to pay it back?

"For everything comes from him and exists by his power and is intended for his glory. All glory to him forever! Amen."

> Intended for what? His glory. Read Isaiah 43:7 (Page 550). What does God say He made us for?

There it is again. *His glory.* This is our purpose: to glorify Him. We can glorify Him in every season or stage of life. Purpose shouldn't be confused with our plans, the roles we play, or feelings of significance. Changes in our status can lead us to question our purpose, but our purpose will always be to glorify God. Worshipping Him is a way to express this glory – even when plans are altered, roles change, or we feel insignificant.

God desires our *lives* to be lived as worship. It's not only something we do for an hour on Sunday or for a few minutes each morning before getting on with our day. It's not just something we do at church. It's not catching some great tune on Christian radio and joining in as we drive to work. Worshipping God should be something we *are*; it's an expression of our purpose.

This life-altering purpose is defined and accomplished internally before being exhibited externally. Glorifying God begins in our mind. When we see God for who He is, we cannot help but worship Him. When we worship Him, our actions begin to exhibit His goodness as well. How do we practically reflect God's glory? For most of us, it's the countless, little ways: through the gift of a smile, a nod of approval, a strong handshake, a hug – simple acts requiring no education, talent, or expertise. The only prerequisite is a transformed life, a life that acknowledges God as the good working through us. When we intentionally discipline ourselves to look to God for the ability to bless others in His name, our practice becomes our character. As God continually receives our attention and credit, our very person, actions, and outlook begin to transform. We must cultivate our desire to worship God as He deserves.

Worship is not a natural state of being. Most often, we decide to ahead of time and then remind ourselves of *Who* we worship as the day unfolds: when we get stuck behind a slow car on our way to an appointment, when the neighbor decides to mow his lawn just as we lie down to nap, when that irritating cough becomes a terrifying symptom – occurrences in our day, big or small, are still grounds for worship. And it's not just the troubling or difficult circumstances that may keep us from worship – it's the good times, the enjoyable pursuits, the happy-go-lucky attitudes that may distract us from worshipping God as well.

> Read together 2 Corinthians 4:18 (Page 884):
> "... We don't look at the troubles we can see now; rather, we fix our gaze on things that cannot be seen. For the things, we see now will soon be gone, but the things we cannot see will last forever."

See, worship keeps daily life in proper perspective. Worship reminds us of our humanity and God's sovereignty.

We spend a great deal of our life measuring ourselves, and others, by what we do. We often measure value by performance. Job titles, bank accounts, children who excel – all these visible measuring sticks can tangle our minds, consume our focus, and determine our behavior. We buy into the idea of worship as being measurable. Since an attitude of worship cannot be measured, it is hard to recognize it as an actual expression of God's glory. Let's see what the Bible says about worship.

> What does Romans 12:1-3 (Page 866) instruct us to do, and why?

Our God-given purpose, superseding any definition of purpose we choose, requires us to give ourselves completely to God. He wants us to serve as His ambassadors throughout the day, regardless of what we're doing or experiencing.

> How does God view such behavior?
> (refer to Romans 12:1-2, Page 866 once again).

Worship requires the internal to inform the external. Our acknowledgment of God and His goodness in our hearts and minds presents itself when we sing, pray, or however we worship Him.

How does this passage say we can cultivate
this internal state of being?

God *transforms* us by changing the way we think! *He* even changes our thought process. It's not something we do; it's something He does. God, who created us in His image, who understands even the mechanics of how we think, who understands our natural tendency to veer toward the negative, gave us the Holy Spirit to live within us and transform our thought process. Christ in us makes it possible for worship to become our *way of life*.

When our thought process is transformed by God's Spirit within us, our perspective changes. Our perspective comes more aligned with God's perspective. We find ourselves praying for the slow driver in front of us and the neighbor mowing his lawn. Our insides don't knot up because our fists are unclenched before God as we focus on all He has done for us and wants us to do for others.

Worship includes thoughts and actions. Further on in Romans 12 we are given more instruction in how to maintain worship as a way of life.

Read Romans 12:9-21 (Page 866) and list the instructions given.

> It's a bit overwhelming, isn't it? Let's break this down.
> Circle the instructions you struggle with the most.

As you do, remind yourself of what you read just before – that God makes every single one of these behaviors possible because His Spirit within you is transforming your thought process! As you continue to look at the challenging behaviors you circled, ask God to help you fully open your mind to His transformative power.

> Now, let's go back and reread the passage. Can you find one single social circumstance left unaddressed?

No. These instructions cover every situation you may face – professionally, socially, personally. It covers every single relationship you have, spousal, parental, casual and close friends, relatives, neighbors, and even enemies. God covers all the bases and presents a true expression of purpose – a purpose that covers every season and circumstance in which you find yourself.

> Just in case you're feeling overwhelmed by the challenge of your circled list, read Philippians 2:13 (Page 900).

God created us, so He gets it. He knows just how difficult the challenge may be for you such as this instance in Martha's life. He works with you. God Himself provides not just the desire, but also the power to do what pleases Him! Does it amaze you to consider the lengths God goes to in helping you accomplish His purpose?

Write down any thoughts you have about
God, yourself, and His purpose for you.

✜

Worshipping God in every season and circumstance reminds us of His complete sovereignty. Sovereignty is the authority or power over a specific area, people, event, or circumstance.

> *Sovereignty is the authority or power over a specific area, people, event, or circumstance.*

Joni Eareckson Tada became a quadriplegic at 17 after a diving accident. Acceptance of her new reality did not come easily, nor did the ability to see her paralysis as an opportunity to worship the Sovereign God who did not prevent the accident, or provide healing afterward. However, once Joni made the decision to fix her focus on God's unlimited abilities rather than her limited ones, doors of unimaginable influence opened for her resulting in the global ministry *Joni and Friends*.

Many years after her accident, I attended an old-fashioned gospel sing Joni hosted at a small church nearby. At its conclusion, she offered to answer any questions. "Ask me anything at all," she encouraged.

A woman raised her hand. "What's the first thing you want to do when you get to heaven?"

Joni thought for a few minutes.

"I honestly hope that when I die I can take my wheelchair with me to heaven," she said. "If I can, I'm going to pick it up and carry it over to Jesus. Then I'm going to lay it at His feet and before He casts it into hell I'm going to say, 'Thank you. Thank you for all the lessons you taught me from this chair.'"

Joni's acceptance of God's sovereignty revealed her life's value. By developing a sense of gratitude, worship became her way of life. As a result, she influences countless people to become transformed by a life-changing relationship with Jesus Christ. It isn't God's answer to Joni's questions (such as "Why?") that gives her the freedom to worship Him, but His sovereignty itself. A trust in God and His goodness drives her life.

Here's the thing. Joni's accident was not necessary for her to live out her God-given purpose. Fulfilling her purpose did not require her paralysis; it only required her trust in God's sovereignty, in His ability to transform any adverse circumstance into something greater than she could possibly imagine.

Nothing in this world can separate us from our loving, sovereign God. Nothing can destroy or detract from our life-purpose. The doors of opportunity to show God's goodness in our corner of the world begin to open around us when we cultivate worship of Him in our lives.

> Read Romans 8:35-39 (Page 863).
>
> What can separate us from God's love?
>
>
>
> As you look at your life right now, what circumstances attempt to make you feel distant from, or ignored by, God?

What can you do to keep things in a truer perspective?

Let God transform your thoughts. Practice making worship consistent as you learn to embrace His sovereignty. Refuse to let your thoughts swerve from the surety of His love for you. When you choose to focus on the wrong you've suffered, the tragedy you've experienced, or the heartache you feel, you will be more aware of pain than of the love of God. It shows. Either way, your pain or His love announces itself to others. Your countenance is not about what's happened to you. It's about *how you entrust to God* what happened to you. God works in you to transform your thought process so what you've experienced will not form destructive scar tissue. His pursuing love brings about emotional health and healing.

> My mother is fighting a losing battle with Alzheimer's. As her brain becomes more compromised by the disease, my grief deepens. It feels unfair. After visiting her one afternoon I sat in my car and wept as I questioned God's love for her. She has trusted you her whole life, through early widowhood, single parenting, the severe brain injury of a child, death of another spouse – why does she now have to suffer this terrible indignity? My thoughts didn't make me feel better. It made me feel ignored by God and hopeless.
>
> To turn my thoughts away from that path and on to the path of worshipping God caused pain; it hurt. In fact, it felt like a sacrifice, which is exactly how the Bible refers to it.

Read Hebrews 13:15 (Page 929).

Sacrifice demands giving up something and sometimes, to worship God, we must sacrifice our bitter or angry feelings and instead worship our Sovereign God who sees and knows what we can't. In this awful circumstance with my mother, I must give up my need for an answer to "Why?" I must have my thoughts transformed to adhere to the truth that God's love for my mother is fully intact and this disease is not separating her from His love.

My struggle in the car that afternoon was fierce, but I forced my thoughts to stay fastened to God the rest of the day, thanking Him for His extravagant love for my mother regardless of how it looked from my limited perspective.

Is there a circumstance in your life right now, or are you in a season, that makes you feel ignored by God? Write down your honest thoughts about it.

Now write a prayer of worship to replace those thoughts and let God begin to transform you.

The next day, at the memory care facility where my mom lives, two care providers stopped to tell me what a blessing she is to other residents. "She's so kind to everyone, making sure they have what they need," one of them said. "She's our ray of sunshine," another told me. "I always feel better around her."

Not only did their words show me God's love was still with my mom, it showed me His love is still shining through her. Even in her extreme disability she is still fulfilling her life-purpose.

Adversity does not equate to an absence of God's love. It does provide an opportunity to bring glory to God as people observe how we navigate our circumstances. This is ambassadorship.

God's sovereign love can turn every circumstance and season into a greater opportunity to fulfill our purpose as we determine to keep our focus on Him and make worship our state of being. When illness limits our productiveness, or our opportunities to use our gifts decline, our purpose does not change, nor does its importance. When circumstances inhibit our availability or retirement changes our status, our purpose doesn't vanish. When our purpose focuses on our internal life that God sees, it produces the added fruit of showing others His goodness.

> *The deepest truth we are all to reveal is the full glory of God, no matter how we feel, who we're with, or what's gone wrong.*[2]
>
> – Emily P. Freeman

In the beginning of his reign, King Solomon of Israel kept his focus on God and God blessed him with great wisdom. But over time, as external influences distracted him from his God-focus, Solomon entered a downward spiral. Despite his vast success and wealth that could buy him anything, his desires became insatiable. He looked elsewhere for fulfillment and elsewhere always disappointed. Solomon's life became an exercise in futility.

In his old age, he recorded his disillusionment in the book of Ecclesiastes. It's difficult to read, especially considering how his life started out, strongly aligned with God and fulfilling his purpose. At the end of his writing he sums up everything with these words: "Here now is my final conclusion: Fear God and obey his commands, for this is everyone's duty" (Ecclesiastes 12:13, Page 511).

Solomon's wisdom was clearly still intact when he wrote those words, but his joy was long gone because his focus had shifted. In Christ, we have abundant life, a rich and satisfying life – a life overflowing with a peace and joy from God Himself (John 10:10, Page 819).

Reflect and Share

This week, observe how you prioritize your time. Take note of your leanings – are you more like Martha or Mary? Were there any distractions that kept you from worshipping God? Be ready to share your experience next time.

Closing Prayer

Father, let my life be a song to You! Each day let me proclaim the good news that You save. Let me tell Your glorious deeds to everyone, all the amazing things You do. In the same way, let my good deeds shine out for all to see, so that everyone will praise You. Let me come close to You, God, so that you will come close to me. Purify my heart so that my loyalty will not be divided between You and the world. You are worthy to receive glory and honor and power. You created all things, and they exist because You created what You pleased. I will be sure to fear You and faithfully serve You as I think of all the wonderful things You have done for me. Amen. (1 Chronicles 16:23, 24, Page 321; Matthew 5:16, Page 736; James 4:8, Page 932; Revelation 4:11, Page 952; 1 Samuel 12:24, Page 219)

In the next few sessions, we'll continue to look at how we can reflect God's glory and fulfill our purpose in each season.

chapter 3

Salt & Light

"You are the light of the world – like a city on a hilltop that cannot be hidden. No one lights a lamp and then puts it under a basket. Instead, a lamp is placed on a stand, where it gives light to everyone in the house. In the same way, let your good deeds shine out for all to see, so that everyone will praise your heavenly Father."

– Matthew 5:14-16 (Page 736)

Mary grew up in a West Virginia holler, always hungry and cold. She and her husband, a laid-off coal miner with black lung disease, struggled to raise their two kids in the same poverty they'd grown up in. But Mary loved Jesus and wanted to be His light in her corner of the world.

Mary heard about a ministry that encourages families to load shoeboxes with small gifts for impoverished children around the world at Christmas. "I see myself in those people," she told the ministry leader later. "I know what they're going through."

She walked from holler to holler, knocking on doors, telling poor people about other poor people, coaxing them to fill a shoebox for the children. By the time she finished, she needed to borrow a 30-foot, 20-ton panel truck to haul 1,200 boxes she'd gathered.

Mary's desire to be a light to her world brightened when the ministry leader invited her to travel internationally to help deliver the shoeboxes.

Mary called the leader announcing, "The President wants me in Washington." She insisted the leader make the trip with her.

Once they entered the Oval Office, Mary took the opportunity to pray for the President. And, she handed an empty shoebox to the President, asking him to fill it.

On the plane to Bosnia, she carried the shoebox filled by the First Family.[3]

When someone sees her overriding expression of purpose as being a light to the world around them, God makes sure the world sees it.

Most children hear this befuddling question: "So what do you want to be when you grow up?" The answers vary: doctor, teacher, nurse, or in the case of my granddaughter, "a full-time scientist and part-time mime." I wonder how Mary answered that question as a hungry little girl shivering in the mountains of West Virginia? Did she dream of growing up to travel the world bringing boxes of "light" to poor children? Probably not. It would have been far beyond her most imaginative dream.

Maybe a better question to ask children would be along the lines of, "So, what kind of person do you want to be when you grow up?" Imagine if right from the beginning of children's lives they were taught about the importance of living out God's purpose for them regardless of the career path they choose. What effect would such a shift in emphasis have on each child, then upon society? An important aspect as a Christian, just like Mary, is to be salt and light – regardless of what purpose we choose for ourselves. If we determine to reflect God's glory, He will direct how far we're sprinkled and how wide we'll shine.

> Read Ephesians 5:8-10 (Page 897).
>
> From where does the light within us come?

God created light. God fills us with *His light*. Think about that for a moment.

"For God, who said, 'Let there be light in the darkness,' has made this light shine in our hearts so we could know the glory of God that is seen in the face of Jesus Christ" (2 Corinthians 4:6, Page 884).

Think about how the sun feels to us after a few days of gray skies.

> Ephesians 5:8-10 (Page 897) reads the light within us produces only what is good and right and true, but the very next verse cautions us to carefully determine what pleases the Lord. Why do you think these verses are connected?

God gives us the gift of the Holy Spirit to live within us.

Read Ephesians 5:15-17 (Page 897-898)
and write a bulleted list of key points.

Being God's light isn't easy. It goes against our nature. That's why we need to be careful. We need to take time to understand what the Lord wants us to do, observe the people we see living a life of light, rather than according to their whims, and then follow suit. These behaviors will magnify His light in us.

The passage concludes by again stressing the importance of praise and thanksgiving as building blocks to keep our thoughts focused on the right things: "... sing psalms and hymns and spiritual songs among yourselves, making music to the Lord in your hearts. And give thanks for everything to God the Father in the name of our Lord Jesus Christ" (Ephesians 5:19-20, Page 898). An attitude of praise and thanksgiving goes hand-in-hand with being light.

From where does both the power and the desire to do what pleases God come? Read Philippians 2:13-15 (Page 900) and note key insights:

Nowhere in the Bible, does God ask, or expect, us to do anything in our own power. At all times, in every circumstance, no matter what, God is willing to do the work in and for us, enabling us to be His light, His shining stars in a dark world.

Let's imagine the account of Deborah, the prophetess in the Bible book of Judges. She probably would have hit it off well with Mary of West Virginia, had they lived during the same period. Like Mary, Deborah aspired to be a light to the people around her. God blessed her with wisdom and insight, so much that people sought her out for advice. In fact, when the judge of Israel died, Deborah's reputation for wise counsel was so well-known she became the next judge.

She took on this responsibility during a very dark period in Israel.

Read Judges 4:1-3 (page 190).

How long had the Israelites suffered oppression and what did they finally do about it?

Does this amaze you? Israel lived in misery for 20 years before its people cried for God to help them! This was not the first time God's people found themselves in dire straits. Their history was to turn away from God, suffer oppression by their enemies, and then cry out to God for relief. God came to their rescue every single time! Why do you think it took them so long to finally turn to God?

How do we see this pattern of delay in our own lives? What's a source of ongoing frustration in your life that you're holding rather than releasing to God?

One amazing characteristic of God is, when we cry out to Him, He responds – just as He did for the Israelites. When we lose sight of our purpose and feel stuck in a pointless existence there's no need to continue wallowing in our misery.

Read the following verses:

Psalm 107:19 (Page 464)

Psalm 91:14-15 (Page 456)

From these verses, who does the Lord rescue?

When does He rescue them?

CHAPTER 3 // SALT & LIGHT

When we call, God *will* answer! His desire and ability to rescue His people weaves, as a theme, throughout the Bible – from Genesis through Revelation. *God wants to rescue us!* Jesus *died* to rescue us! Endless verses reassure us that God will respond to our cries for help. This is exactly what happened during Deborah's period of judgeship.

> Continue reading her story in Judges 4:4-7 (Pages 190-191).
>
> God hears our cry for help! Whatever you wrote down as your ongoing source of frustrations and heartache, take a moment right now and ask God for help. Take a few minutes to write out your prayer.
>
> Now we come to a fun part of Deborah's story. Read Judges 4:8-9 (Page 191).
>
> What does God draw your attention to in this passage?

Barak wasn't about to go into a battle where the odds were stacked against him unless Deborah, a woman, was at his side. Deborah, who

51

was fully up to the challenge, made sure Barak understood the credit for the victory would not be going to him. It would go to a woman!

One exquisite truth woven into this wonderful story is that while most every culture has valued one gender or race over another, God doesn't. While His individual plan for each of us is unique, His *purpose* for us is the same: proclaim His glory. Be salt and light.

In her childhood dreams, Deborah probably never imagined herself as a great military leader, let alone a judge! Most women were the home-tenders in her day, the baby-producers. And some worked the fields. But her amazing story, recounted in Judges 4-5, again shows us that when our focus is on our God-given purpose to reflect God's glory, there is no limit to how far our light will shine.

> **Along with being light, God asks us to be salt. Note what the following verses say:**
>
> **Matthew 5:13 (Page 736)**
>
>
>
> **Colossians 4:6 (Page 904)**

Salt serves two purposes: it preserves and it enhances flavor. The Holy Spirit within us preserves the goodness of God within us – it enables us to overcome evil as our God-influenced behavior and speech enhances the flavor of life. As people around us watch us respond to challenges,

CHAPTER 3 // SALT & LIGHT

interact with our families and others, conduct business, an observable difference should give them pause, causing them to wonder and perhaps in time, believe.

> According to Matthew 5:13 (Page 736), what effect does it have when people who profess to be Christ-followers behave in opposition to God's principles?

They are no longer good for anything! Chilling words, indeed. It's of infinite importance as followers of Christ that we do not in any way detract from Him. He promises to give us both the desire and the power to live in a way that glorifies Him in every circumstance and every season. We are without excuse.

> According to Colossians 4:6 (Page 904), what is the stipulation put on our speech?

Always gracious! Always seasoned with life-enhancing flavor! It's no coincidence that speech and salt are connected in this passage. Words have immense capacity to both build up and tear down. So often our careless words tear down. Words cannot be called back once spoken. This brings us again to the importance of worship. We want the God of our internal attitude to govern our external behaviors and even the words we speak.

53

Read the following verses and summarize:

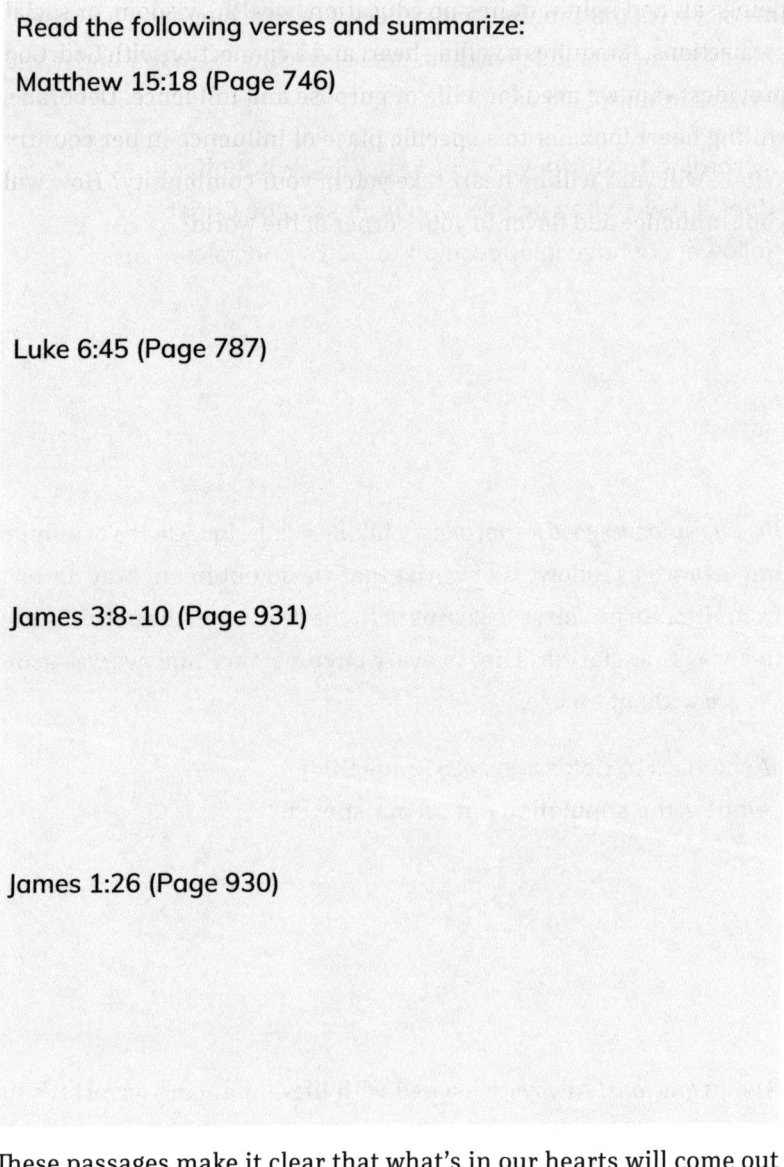

Matthew 15:18 (Page 746)

Luke 6:45 (Page 787)

James 3:8-10 (Page 931)

James 1:26 (Page 930)

These passages make it clear that what's in our hearts will come out from our lips. The two are inseparable. The only way to be salt to the people around us is by keeping our hearts fused to God. We need to make it our driving purpose to bring Him glory in all we say and do.

Being salt and light requires no education, wealth, wisdom, or social connections. It requires a willing heart and a connection with God. God provides what we need for a life of purpose and influence. Deborah's willing heart took her to a specific place of influence in her country. Where will your willing heart take you in your community? How will your influence add flavor to your corner of the world?

Reflect and Share

Consider your schedule this week. Below, write three places where you might have the opportunity to share the light of Christ. Pray about it!

Closing Prayer

Father, I acknowledge You are the light of the world and Your light shines everywhere. Don't let me hide my light but let me shine like a city on a hilltop. Let what I do shine out for all to see so that everyone will praise You. Let me also be like salt that never loses flavor, loving my enemies, doing good to them, lending without expecting to be repaid, showing compassion just as You are compassionate. Don't let me judge or condemn others. Help me to forgive as You have forgiven me. I know the temptations in my life are no different from what others experience. I know You are faithful and will not allow the temptation to be more than I can stand. Thank You that when I am tempted You always show me a way out so that I can endure. God, You are light, and there is no darkness in You at all. Help me to live in Your light and I thank You for the blood of Jesus, Your Son, that has cleansed me from all sin. Amen. (Matthew 5:14-16, Page 736; Luke 6:35-36, Page 786; 1 Corinthians 10:13, Page 876; 1 John 1:5,7, Page 941)

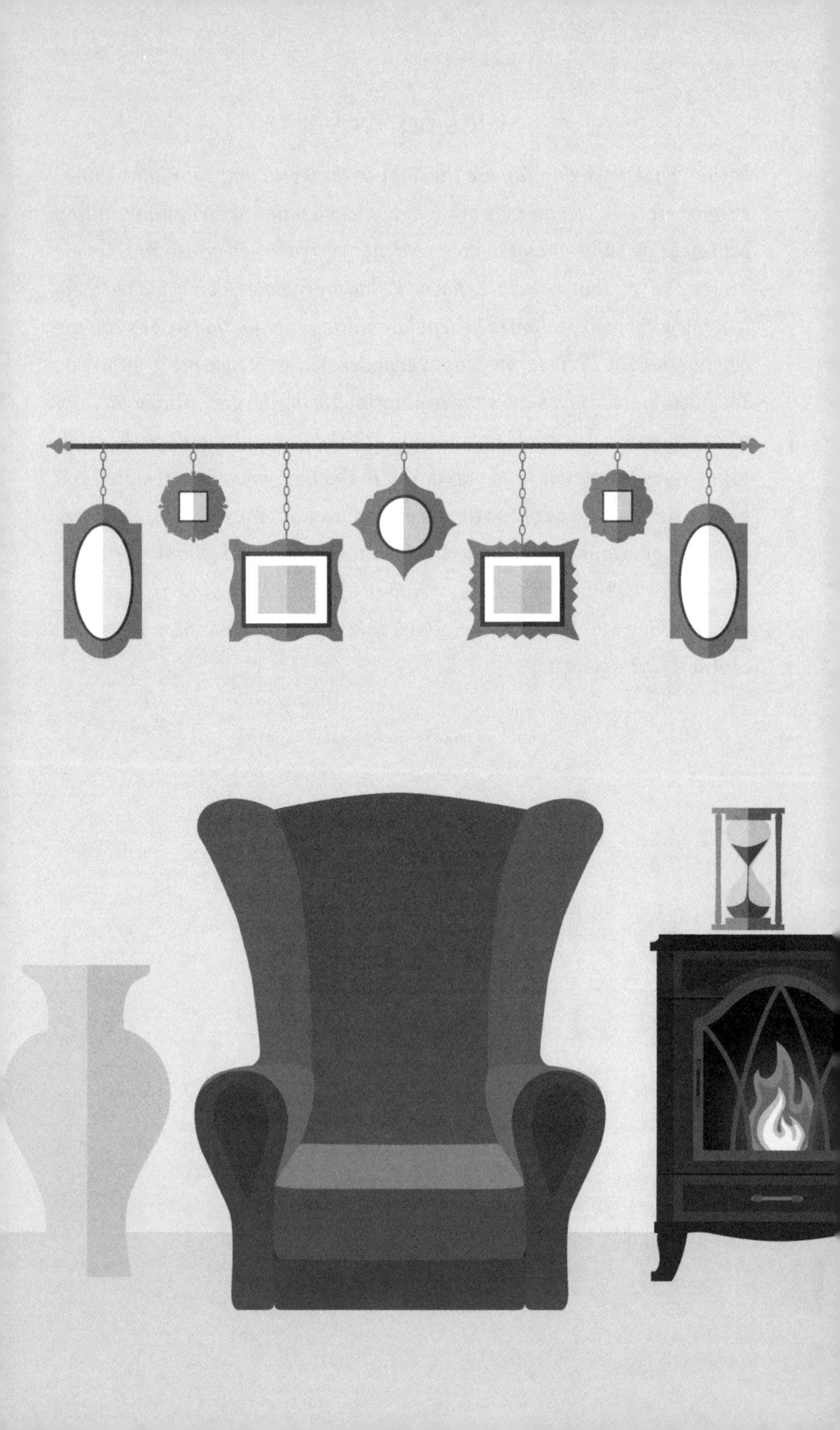

chapter 4

Trust God

"Don't be afraid, for I am with you. Don't be discouraged, for I am your God. I will strengthen you and help you. I will hold you up with my victorious right hand."

– Isaiah 41:10 (Page 548)

The late John Kavanaugh, noted ethicist and longtime member of St. Louis University's department of philosophy, taught and wrote on the practical application of ethics. At one point in his life he felt the need to gain a clearer perspective on things. He admitted a lack of direction on how to spend the rest of his life. So, to gain clarity he decided to spend some time in Calcutta working alongside Mother Teresa as she ministered to India's poor and dying. One day, as they worked together, he asked her to pray for him.

"What do you want me to pray for?" she asked him.

He then uttered the request he had carried across the ocean, for thousands of miles: "Clarity," he said. "Pray that I have clarity."

Mother Teresa's response took him aback. "No, I will not do that," she said. "Clarity is the last thing you are clinging to and must let go of."

Kavanaugh didn't understand her reply because she seemed to have such great clarity, the very kind he was looking for. When he asked about it, she laughed. "I have never had clarity; what I have always had is trust. So, I will pray that you trust God."[4]

In what season or circumstance in your life are you asking for more of God?

When it comes to a desire for purpose in a specific season of life, we can get our priorities wrong. Wouldn't it be great to have the clarity you seek appear in tangible form – a flashing neon arrow pointing toward the path on the left, or maybe even a heavenly text? An undefined reason for life carries a weight to it that only lightens with clarity. We desire to feel a sense of significance regardless of the season we're in, or how many years we've accumulated.

When it comes to aging, sometimes the effort to stay in the current of life becomes daunting as our culture keeps nudging us closer to shore where the water is becalmed and safe.

When we ask for clarity or direction, we ask for something from God – for Him to grant us a thing. When we ask for more of God, we ask Him for more of what He desires to give – more of Himself.

Here, in pools of stagnancy, clarity of significance can feel as necessary as air. Everyone needs a reason to get up in the morning. Chances are that reason isn't going to be texted to us. When we put first things first – seeking more of God – our steps will be lit. "Your word is a lamp to guide my feet and a light for my path" (Psalm 119:105, Page 470).

Mother Teresa understood that clarity gets in the way of trust. When our top desire is to find clarity, life gets complicated. Poling about muddies the water, keeping us from moving in any direction at all. Focusing on God simplifies, leaves us with one choice to contemplate: to trust or not trust.

Read Proverbs 3:5-6 (Page 482) and summarize:

What do these verses tell us not to do?

When making important decisions we always consider the pros and cons, don't we? We talk to people with experience or expertise. We research. These are wise things to do, but the truth is, no matter how well-informed our decision is today, we have no idea how it will play out tomorrow. Only God possesses a future perspective. How many people in the Bible seemed to take a wrong turn, only to have God produce good? What looks like a wise decision today may turn out to be not so good after all. What may appear incorrect may be the place of trust!

> The rest of this passage offers us additional wisdom.
> Read it again, out loud.

Did you notice a tiny repeated word? Trust with *all* your heart. Seek His will in *all* ways. When our trust rests in God, our worry about making the right decision dissipates – He receives glory. His omniscience leads us. His goodness guides us. God knows the future. If things don't go as we expect, we still trust that God remains active and present, working in all circumstances to strengthen us and make us more reflective of the Holy Spirit in us – which needs to be our ultimate goal, regardless of the path we walk.

> What is the common theme of the following verses?
>
> Proverbs 16:3 (Page 492)
>
> Psalm 121:3 (Page 472)
>
> Psalm 9:10 (Page 417)

God will show you the way to go. Whatever happens on your path, *you will be successful.* God's definition of success is different than ours. In baseball, success is measured by batting average, wins and losses, strikeouts, and home runs. You can go to Cooperstown, New York, and read the definitions of success on each of the Hall of Famers' plaques

CHAPTER 4 // TRUST GOD

there. God doesn't measure batting average for His Hall of Fame. Read Hebrews 11 (Pages 926-927). The entire chapter starts with the word that defines success.

> Write it in capital letters here:

Even when your decision does not turn out the way you expect, if you trust God, you succeed. Why? Because He always has your best interest in mind. You will not stumble! Trusting God never leads us in the wrong direction because the intentional discipline of trust keeps us focused on Him, not our circumstances. That in turn, keeps our mind fully open to God's input.

> Read the following:
>
> Isaiah 26:3 (Page 535)
>
> Philippians 4:6-7 (Page 901)
>
> What is the result of a mind fixed on God rather than circumstances?

Isn't that what we truly desire? Absolute and perfect peace – wherever we are, whatever's going on around us. God's peace overpowers our fears, soothes our mind. The result of this is exactly what John Kavanaugh sought. He said his aim was clarity, but the root of that clarity is trust.

Let's read the story of Mary, the mother of Jesus, through one person's perspective. This is not exact to the biblical account, but may give you an idea of how one woman imagined her life:

Mary was probably in her teens when God revealed His daunting plan for her life: give birth to and raise His only Son, Jesus Christ. Can you imagine the lightning bolts of shocked questions that struck her mind after the angel's visit? How desperately she must have clung to those first words the heavenly messenger spoke to her: "Greetings favored woman! The Lord is with you!" (Luke 1:28, Page 779). When fear and shame may have tried to capture her thoughts, how those words must have soothed her wonderings. *God was with her; she was favored!* As pieces of her life map kept breaking off, these words must have reassured her. *God was with her; she was favored.*

For Mary, from that point on, trusting God became a discipline that could constantly be challenged. Did it ever leave her mind for even a moment that she was raising God in human form? Did she ever obsess about her ability to parent *God? And do it well?* What about when Jesus' earthly ministry began and people rejected Him and plotted to kill Him? How did she handle that as a mother? How arduously did she have to rely on God to guard her thoughts so as not to become bitter and resentful toward her son's enemies? Did she ever scream out to God, "Why aren't You doing something? This is Your Son! Don't You see how they're treating Him?" What about the day of His arrest and fatal crucifixion? As she stood at the foot of His cross, witnessing His unspeakable pain, how difficult was it to keep her eyes fixed on God?

We are given no indication that Mary strayed from her trust in God. When life leads us through unbearable seasons, our determined trust in God, our intentional focus on Him, will keep our minds protected and produce a peace beyond understanding (Philippians 4:6-7, Page 901): "Don't worry about anything; instead, pray about everything. Tell God what you need and thank him for all he has done. Then you will experience God's peace, which exceeds anything we can understand.

His peace will guard your hearts and minds as you live in Christ Jesus." He keeps our life's significance intact.

> Read the following verses:
>
> Psalm 32:8 (Page 427)
>
> Psalm 37:23 (Page 430)
>
> What does God tell you as you read these verses?
>
>
>
>
> How do these words feel true and applicable based on your current circumstances?
>
>
>
>
> Do you feel like you are on the best pathway, that you are living out your purpose? Why or why not?

Every day when I walk through the door of the memory care facility where my mom lives I must place a stubborn guard around my thoughts with Bible verses such as these. From my perspective, this does not feel like the best pathway for my mom's life or mine. I can't figure out what her fulfillment of purpose might be in this final season of her life and see no detail that is delight-worthy. *But God says He delights in every detail* so I set my mind to trust that He delights in how my mom and I walk this pathway. And sometimes, when I take her hand to pray and hear comprehensible and heartfelt words of gratitude coming from her lips, then for a second I, too, feel delight and peace and it is enough – because God is enough, just as He promised.

Our ability to trust God is sometimes tied to our thought process. Our thoughts, even our subconscious thoughts, can control our emotions and our emotions sometimes control our responses. To strengthen our ability to trust God, we need to practice intentionality.

Read the following verses and note what they say to do.

Romans 8:5-6 (Page 862)

Colossians 3:2 (Page 903)

Philippians 4:8 (Page 901)

Don't forget – God said He will transform the way you think. Keep reminding yourself His Spirit lives within you. No matter what's happening, make the conscious effort to look to God and do not focus on your circumstances. Fix your mind on what is true, good, pure, and beautiful. There is your purpose: Glorify God through the focus of your thoughts.

Lynn was a single woman who worked for the same company nearly 30 years. Then, as things often change, her corporation reorganized,

CHAPTER 4 // TRUST GOD

and Lynn found herself unemployed – in a new life season.

Life threw Lynn a curve. She left her final workday feeling a tornado of emotions as she drove home in silence. Of course, there were the scary thoughts – including no spouse to rely on for financial or emotional support. Would she make the right decisions? Would she head down the path she was supposed go? Had she wasted 30 years at this job?

When have you faced a season of uncertainty?

List the various paths you considered when you faced an uncertain future. It's OK. You can list the not-so-happy ones!

For Lynn, the choices seemed simple. She could wallow in sadness over her long career and the friends she would leave behind, or she could embrace this new season and look forward to what God planned for her future.

Lynn soon felt a peace about the situation. The reality was that her life was not over; this ending was a new beginning – a new direction. In the meantime, she eased into a time of rest.

From that moment, Lynn decided to make every effort to take the positive route. Instead of the scary questions, she chose to think about the options: first, to decide what she wanted to do with her life between now and retirement by identifying what genuinely made her happy and second, to determine the legacy she would like to leave behind. She knew it was time to reevaluate where she was in life, her God-given gifts, and recall what her success looks like through God's eyes.

Lynn allowed herself a time of adjustment, a time to "be still" and listen to the Holy Spirit. She filled her days with worship music and the Bible. She took her thoughts captive, pushing away from the negative and focusing on the future God would direct for her life.

Lynn loved shopping the vintage booths at the local antique shop, so she decided to lease a booth to occupy her mind and hands during the transition. It was an item on her bucket list – *so why not make a little money while she waited for her life answer?* The booth was a wonderful experience, including warm, new friends and encouragement from the shop owner for her creative gifts. It filled many of Lynn's days with direction and gave her the season of respite she needed.

Before long, Lynn found herself working full time at a women's outreach ministry using both her creative gifts and the skills she obtained in the corporate world. God put her on a path to glorify Him.

While we don't have control over the thoughts that flit into our minds, we have absolute control over which thoughts hang around and take root. Refusing to subject every thought to God will exponentially decrease your ability to trust Him.

Strive to remember the times God delivered you, the times He brought you through the wilderness, the times He comforted you and gave you the ability to focus on Him rather than your circumstances.

According to the following passages, what habit should you form?

Psalm 59:16 (Pages 439-440)

1 Chronicles 16:9 (Page 321)

Psalm 63:6 (Page 441)

"Never stop praying," Paul wrote to the Thessalonians. "Be thankful in all circumstances, for this is God's will for you who belong to Christ Jesus" (1 Thessalonians 5:17-18, Page 907).

Morning, noon, and night decide to fill your thoughts with praise. Begin each day acknowledging God and His very personal love for you. Throughout the day think and talk about all He has done. Meditate on Him during wakeful moments of the night. Protect your mind with an attitude of praise and trust.

The third very helpful habit is found in Psalm 119:11 (Page 468).

Memorizing Scripture takes the words off the page of your Bible and plants them in your heart so you are never without the guidance of God's Word. He will bring the words you memorize to mind the very moment you need them.

It's easy to discount the value of memorization – especially as we age. The words don't stick as easily as they once did. It can feel like an exercise in futility, but it is not! The discipline of memorization is even more essential to our well-being as we age. God's Word keeps our thoughts on track. He sees our efforts and what we think we've forgotten will come back to us when we need it.

With God's Word in our hearts and His praises in our mouths, trust becomes a more consistent state – and trust brings glory to God!

Reflect and Share

Ask the Lord to recall a worship song that will stay with you and keep you focused on His trustworthiness and faithfulness to guide you through anything that concerns you right now. Write the words of the song below:

_____
_____
_____
_____
_____
_____
_____
_____
_____
_____
_____
_____
_____
_____
_____
_____
_____
_____
_____
_____

Closing Prayer

Father, Your unfailing love is better than life itself; how I praise you! I will praise You as long as I live, lifting up my hands to You in prayer. I will not worry about anything today but I will pray instead, telling You what I need and thanking You for all You have done. Thank You for the peace You give me that exceeds anything I can understand as it guards my heart and my mind. I will let Your peace rule my heart because You have called me to live in peace and I will always be thankful. I will praise You at all times and I will constantly speak Your praises. Thank You for Your voice whispering in my ear, "This is the way you should go," whether to the right or to the left. I am so grateful for Your promise to never leave me or let me be alone. Amen. (Psalm 63:3-4, Page 441; Philippians 4:6-7, Page 901; Colossians 3:15, Page 904; Psalm 34:1, Page 428; Isaiah 30:21, Pages 539-540; Hebrews 13:5, Page 928)

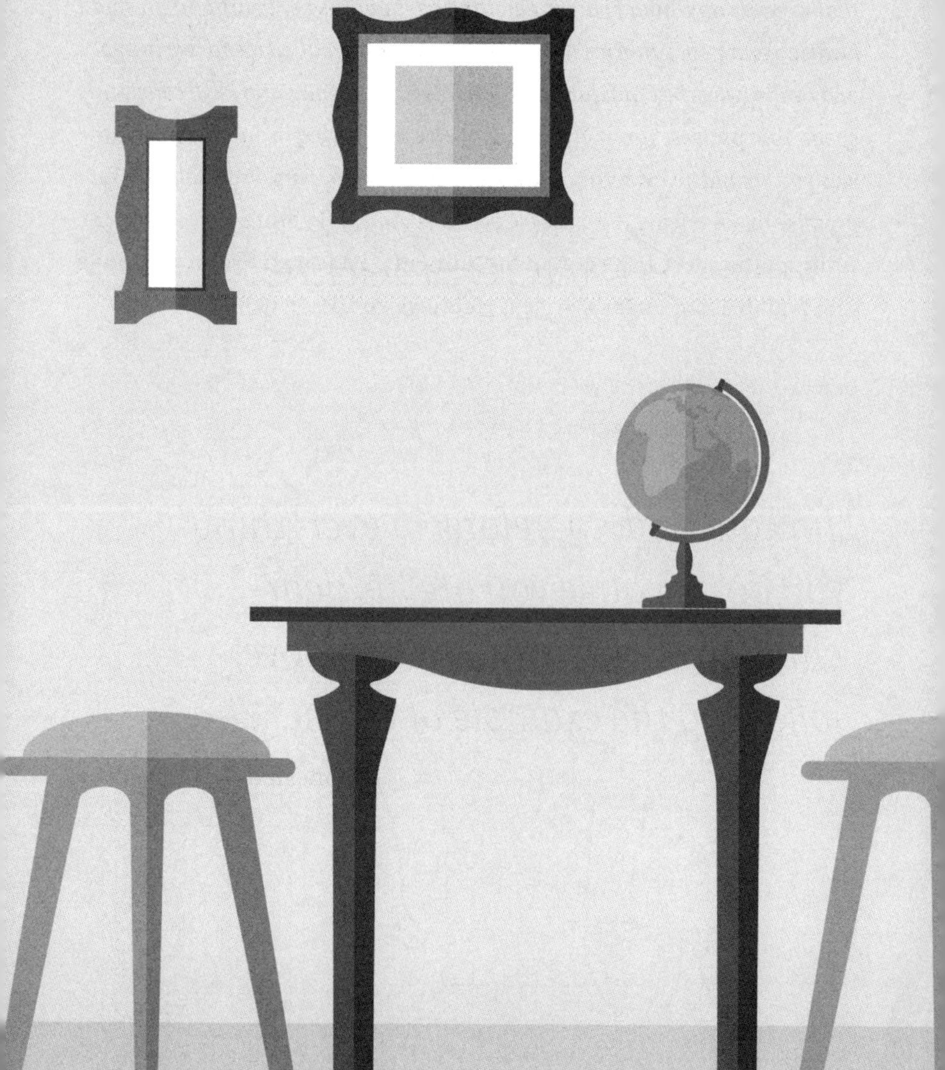

chapter 5

Be His Image-Bearer

"Imitate God, therefore, in everything you do, because you are his dear children. Live a life filled with love, following the example of Christ. ..."

– Ephesians 5:1-2 (Page 897)

After she was widowed at 32, Zell's role immediately shifted to finding a means of supporting her three young children. Five years and two college degrees later, she entered the classroom for the first time as the teacher. The years that followed were busy ones, raising her family and teaching. In time her children grew up and one by one left home to begin their own lives. When her last child married, she took a deep breath and looked around, realizing that for the first time since her husband's death, her life wasn't tied to providing for her family. She could go in whatever direction she wanted.

A few years later she met a widowed dairy farmer and decided she wanted nothing more than to join him in the dairy business. They were married surrounded by their six adult children. Zell had grown up on a farm and delighted in once again being knee-deep in the hard but satisfying work of farming. Zell and Don had been married one brief year when a midnight phone call changed everything once again. Don's oldest daughter had been struck by a drunk driver. Her injuries were severe, and permanent. She required care the rest of her life.

Now, in addition to farming – a role Zell chose eagerly – a new duty forced itself into her life: the all-consuming, exhausting exercise of caregiver for a brain-injured adult. She did have a choice though: duty or love? Duty was required of her. Love became her expression of purpose.

Sometimes, we define our purpose, born out of our interests and opportunities. Some thrive on challenges presented and pursue specific goals and remain motivated by the possibilities. Sometimes we make choices to simply survive and provide. Other times an unasked for and unwelcomed role appears in our path. Maybe it arrives in the form of a death or the end of a marriage. Perhaps purpose is wrapped in health challenges or some other event that changes the course of our lives for a season or forever.

These unchosen plans profoundly affect every aspect of our being and must somehow be managed in the mix of the path we're already walking. Sometimes it throws a barricade up that blocks our path forever. When we must rearrange our life, putting things we value on hold, how do we find our sense of true purpose?

We may ask, *Why would God allow these circumstances into our lives?* To find answers we must rely again on trust – we must believe God has the interest and power to use our broken heart and destroyed dreams to grow, even enhance, our relationship with Him and others. We must trust in this circumstance, He will lay out a different life plan we can come to cherish and find fulfillment within. God leverages our tragedies and heartaches in ways we never imagined. He can help us find ways to glorify Him in our pain.

> Read 2 Corinthians 4:6-7 (Page 884) and note here what it says about the light of God:

Think for a moment about the light God created. In the day, it is always visible to some degree, regardless of the time or the weather. Even during the stormiest of nights when the stars and moon are invisible, there is often an illumination behind the clouds preventing total darkness. This constantly changing intensity of light is essential to life – and it's similar to the light that indwells followers of Christ! Ever-present. Illuminating. Never subservient to darkness.

> Now read 2 Corinthians 4:8-10 (Page 884).
> Note phrases that stand out to you.

God's light, that cannot be extinguished, overcomes any dark circumstance that enters your life. As bad as the circumstance might be, it cannot crush you, drive you to despair, destroy you, or cause God to abandon you. You can be sure that whatever circumstance alters the course of your life, it's not the result of God abandoning you or pushing you away. He holds you in His hands, one over the other, tightly clasped together. ("Don't be afraid, for I am with you. Don't be discouraged, for I am your God. I will strengthen you and help you. I will hold you up with my victorious right hand" – Isaiah 41:10, Page 548.)

> According to 2 Corinthians 4:10 (Page 884),
> what is one reason we suffer?

We keep coming back to it, don't we? Our purpose in every circumstance is to make Jesus visible to everyone around us, to be His image-bearer. This glorifies God.

> According to 2 Corinthians 4:18 (Page 884), how
> can we focus on our purpose in circumstances that
> take us in a direction we don't want to go?

Choosing where we will fix our gaze makes all the difference. Will we stare disappointedly at what is temporary, or joyfully gaze on what is eternal – on our unchosen circumstance or on God?

Let's consider another woman named Mary in the Bible. I imagine her story goes something like this:

> Mary was a woman who knew well the importance of a right focus. She lived an enviable life of wealth and influence until circumstances beyond her control took it all away. Accosted with an extreme mental affliction that would hit without warning, she became a laughingstock in her community. Sometimes her behavior grew so volatile people feared for their safety around her. Parents probably warned their children to keep their distance.
>
> Think about her life when a man named Jesus visited her community of Magdala. As He walked down the street, a commotion drew his attention. Coming closer, He saw Mary, hollowed eyes, sunken cheeks, raving madly as the crowd around her jeered. But Jesus didn't see the woman the crowd jeered at – He saw the woman who'd been created in His Father's image and He felt immense compassion. He made His way through the circle of people and approached her. Her haunted eyes raised to meet His and light at last dawned in her soul. Her mental torment calmed and never returned.
>
> In her immeasurable gratitude, from that day forward, she began to live her life around His. She followed Jesus and His disciples as they traveled, taking care of them, supporting Jesus' ministry. It wasn't easy, but it rewarded her with a reason for her life. Her love for God drove her focus and her actions. She probably worried about the growing controversy surrounding Him, aware that some very powerful people wanted Him stopped. Not knowing what else to do, she simply stayed close, in the background, doing whatever needed to be done.

Then one terrible night, in one of the most peaceful spots of all Jerusalem, a cadre of soldiers entered the garden where Jesus had gone to pray. They arrested Him and took Him to the high priest. The next hours passed in a blur of torture and pain. There was the obscene mockery (Mary knew well that feeling), the cruel beating, the farce of a trial, and finally the terrible march through the city as Jesus carried His own cross, until He could no longer. Through it all, Mary kept her faith fixed on her Savior, refusing to doubt, saying no to indifference, continuing to follow even as her heart felt it would explode from the horror. She stood watching as He took His last breath; she felt the ground tremble violently beneath her feet as the very world He'd created rebelled against the events of the day. *Nothing could draw her away.*

Mary stayed at the site of the crucifixion until Jesus' body was taken down and then she accompanied it to the tomb donated by one of His supporters. She waited until the body was laid inside and a huge stone rolled across the opening before she went home to prepare the spices for His burial. Her whole being was numbed. *What on earth would she do? Her entire existence had just been put in a tomb.*

Let's pause the story. Write about a time when you felt like life stood still.

We'll continue with Mary's story. Days later, early and while it was still dark, Mary headed back to the tomb. We can imagine her grief and confusion kept her mind in turmoil all night. She was exhausted. She wouldn't ever be able to roll away the heavy stone covering the tomb's entrance. Still, she went. Perhaps one of the soldiers ordered to guard the tomb would help. When she arrived, she was bewildered to see the stone rolled back – and Jesus' body gone! She fled back to the disciples. "They've taken His body!" she yelled. "We don't know where they've put Him!"

Peter and another disciple (possibly John) ran to the tomb to see for themselves. Mary followed breathlessly behind. *Indeed, the tomb was empty.* Perplexed, not knowing what to do, the men returned. Mary stayed, weeping inconsolably.

Read John 20:11-18 (Page 828) and note the details that followed.

This passage portrays such deep sorrow, doesn't it? The disciples have returned home and Mary is alone at the tomb with a grief so intense she can't think of anything but what her eyes are telling her, her circumstances: *someone has stolen her beloved Teacher's body!* She is too distraught to see there is something unusual about the two men in white robes who appear at the tomb. When she steps out of the tomb, she begs the man she assumes to be the gardener to tell her where they've taken the body. She is so utterly consumed with sorrow she doesn't recognize Jesus. *Alive! In front of her.*

So often our greatest significance is revealed through our greatest pain – when our life map lays broken at our feet. The role Mary joyfully filled – supporting Jesus – was violently taken away. Then something inconceivable happens. Jesus utters one word, and everything changes.

EVERY SEASON: EMBRACING A FOREVER KIND OF PURPOSE

> According to John 20:16 (Page 828), what is that word?

Mary hears *her* name come from her Savior's lips and instantly she recognizes Him. Oh, just imagine that moment! Imagine the extreme reversal of emotion – from unspeakable sorrow to indescribable joy! As you imagine that moment, imagine Jesus saying your name.

> Write your name out slowly as you do this. Share your thoughts.

Here is the truth: Jesus *is* saying your name, and your name on Jesus' lips changes everything! His resurrection offers you an eternal purpose that supersedes all others – to proclaim His life and salvation!

Jesus chose Mary to be the first person He appeared to. Why not influential Peter, one of the best-known disciples, who had just been at the tomb? Why not John or any of the other more logical choices? *Why Mary of Magdala?* There's no concrete answer to this question – only wonder at the beauty of His choice – a woman, once so damaged then transformed by Jesus' love. A woman whose purpose began when she met Jesus, continued as He died, then elevated when He rose from the dead. In a very real sense Mary represents each one of us, desperately in need of transformation, searching for purpose – discovering it can only be found in Jesus and His Good News.

> When my time began to be taken up more and more with the care of my mother and her sister, I was also caring for my granddaughter who was then a 2-year-old. One day, I buckled and unbuckled Milo into her car seat 16 times as I drove my mom

and aunt around to various appointments and errands. That night, wearied in body and spirit, I sank into bed. All I could see ahead of me were days exactly like this one. *This is not the way I want to spend the rest of my life!* My advancing years fueled a sense of urgency. My opportunity to do things I wanted to do was rapidly disappearing. As passionately as I loved my granddaughter, mother, and aunt, this did not seem like the best use of my shrinking years of productivity. *But what option did I have?*

In his devotional blog, *Living a Life of Service*, Rick Warren writes, "There are three things you can do with your life: You can waste it, you can spend it, or you can invest it. The best use of your life is to invest your life in something that will outlast it. The worst thing you can do is to live simply for today and to live for yourself. God did not put you on Earth to live for yourself. He created you to be like Christ."[5]

> *I don't believe there is one great thing I was made to do in this world. I believe there is one great God I was made to glorify. And there will be many ways, even a million little ways, I will declare his glory with my life.*[6]
>
> – Emily P. Freeman

Do your current circumstances make you feel like your life is spent running errands for other people, caring for aging family members, fulfilling tasks for which others are too busy? Do you feel like your time is being used up more than invested? Are you consumed with activities that keep you busy, but not with important action? Consider this: If you are being God's image-bearer in all you are doing, then you are fulfilling your key purpose – reflecting His glory. Stop viewing what you're doing as simply *spending* your life; see it as an investment.

Read the following and note the key instruction for us:

1 Timothy 6:18-19 (Page 913)

Galatians 6:2, 9-10 (Page 894)

Titus 3:14 (Page 918)

Do these verses sound like a list of errands to you? Helping people can start to feel like just another task. This happens when we focus on what we'd rather be doing instead of focusing on bringing glory to God. But what do these verses reveal that is really being accomplished?

Storing up for the future. Laying groundwork for true life. Reaping a harvest of blessing. Being productive. In another word – investing! When done with the right focus, everything you do to help others is investing in eternity.

Read Matthew 6:19–21 (Page 737).

This passage references our money and possessions, but a bigger lesson can be applied. Helping others with any motive other than being God's image-bearer is nothing more than storing up treasures here on Earth, running errands. Those investments are short-lived. If your heart's desire is to bear God's image, then everything you do becomes an investment He, Himself, will multiply.

> When Zell found her entire day, every day, being eaten away with the care of her stepdaughter, she knew she had two choices: fight it in bitterness or embrace it with trust in God to guide her steps day by day. She chose the latter. Her verses for survival became Philippians 4:12-14 (Page 901):
>
> "I know how to live on almost nothing or with everything. I have learned the secret of living in every situation, whether it is with a full stomach or empty, with plenty or little. For I can do everything through Christ, who gives me strength. Even so, you have done well to share with me in my present difficulty."
>
> Zell fused her identity to God. He made her who she was – a fragile human vessel with spectacular means of displaying the light of God as she lived out her God-given purpose. As one family member said, "She is an angel from God to our family."

At some point most everyone faces an unwelcome, uninvited circumstance at the door to her life. Often it barges right in. When that happens, be confident that God will offer you the opportunity to live out His high purpose for you right within those circumstances. What you do with that offer remains up to you, but you will never regret accepting God's offer, using the circumstance to let God's light shine even brighter through you.

Reflect and Share

Write a note to someone who is facing a difficult circumstance. Encourage her with the truth that God loves her (use a Bible verse or your own words) and let her know you are praying for her.

Closing Prayer

Father, I don't want to live only to satisfy my own sinful nature but to live to please Your Spirit and harvest everlasting life. Help me not get tired of doing what is good, looking forward to reaping at just the right time a harvest of blessing if I don't give up. Let me take the opportunity to do good to everyone – especially to those in the family of faith. Lord, I see how very much You love me, because You call me Your child and that is what I am! I am eager for the day when You appear and I will be fully like You, seeing You as You really are. Because of this eager expectation help me keep myself pure, just as You are pure. Don't let me just say I love others but let me show my love by my actions so I am confident when I at last stand before You. Amen. (Galatians 6:8-10, Page 894; 1 John 3:1-3, 18-19, Page 942)

"When you produce a lovely vase, you are my best designer. This time a great one, again." *Faber*

chapter 6

Bear Fruit

"When you produce much fruit, you are my true disciples. This brings great glory to my Father."

– John 15:8 (Page 824)

Imagine this scene with me:

It was a day like every other. Get up, get dressed, start working through the daily to-dos. Like all days when something unexpected happens, she expected nothing out of the ordinary that day. She watched the sun, wanting to go fill her water jugs around midday when no one else would likely use the community well. Her timing was not due to courtesy, but to avoid embarrassment. She just didn't want to deal with anyone and their cutting remarks or judgmental glances.

As the sun reached its zenith, she hefted the water jug to her shoulder and headed toward the edge of town to the well. The midday heat, thick with dust, pushed in around her. She loosened her headscarf to allow more airflow. Approaching the well, she was startled to see a man waiting alone. She could see he was a Jew and hesitated for a moment, unsure what to do; Jews were known to hold prejudice against her people. Then it happened.

He spoke to her.

"Please give me a drink."

Taken aback, she blurted, "You are a Jew, and I am a Samaritan woman. Why are you asking me for a drink?"

The discussion that followed became the most fascinating she'd ever had. *This was no typical man sitting here!*

Suddenly, the conversation became more personal, and to her shock she heard herself telling him she was single. Without missing a beat, the man replied, "You're right! You don't have a husband – for you have had five husbands, and you aren't even married to the man you're living with now" (John 4:17-18, Page 812).

Even as she tried to figure out how He could possibly know this, they switched topics again, this time to religious beliefs. What He said confused her, so she reverted to what she knew all Jews would agree. "I know the Messiah is coming – the one who is called Christ. When He comes, He will explain everything" (John 4:25, Page 812).

The very next words from His mouth would change her life forever. What was His reply in John 4:26 (Page 812)?

The Messiah! The very one she waited for – *Jesus Christ*. Standing before her. In the flesh. It was the last thing she'd expected to hear Him say but it made all the pieces of their conversation fit into place, including His knowledge of her past and present. Her chest pounded as transformational truth began to dawn upon her heart. She forgot all about the water. Leaving her jug in the dust beside the well, she ran back to her village.

Read John 4:28-30 (Page 812) and note here what happens:

When something big happens, we want to tell everyone, don't we? We can't hold the news in and this woman had just experienced something big! She feels no hesitancy, no shyness, no concern over how people might respond. As slowly and cautiously as she approached the well earlier, she quickly ran back into the village to spread her Good News, wanting everyone to meet the Man she had just met.

According to John 4:39-42 (Page 812), what happened?

Her encounter with Jesus produced fruit. It brought God glory. She discovered her purpose! Did you catch the definitive phrases? *Many of the Samaritans. A lot more people.* What had been her own personal experience, the villagers now experienced for themselves: *they believed in Jesus.* In her excitement, the woman became God's ambassador.

The necessity and urgency to bear fruit is woven throughout the Bible. God created the magnificent plan of eternal life for all who believe in Him – and then placed this plan in our fallible hands. Regardless of our personality styles, talents, passions, capabilities, and education levels, God designed and called each of us to produce fruit and multiply.

Sharing this Good News – that Jesus Christ died for our sins and is alive – is our daily, God-designed purpose. Bearing fruit glorifies God. This expression should be woven into all the other roles and ways we find significance throughout the changing seasons of our lives. It's our expression of purpose as we build a career and when we retire from one, while raising a family and while babysitting grandkids. It gives God glory during seasons of celebration, loneliness, grief, illness, and health. It's there when nothing is happening and when too much is happening, in business relationships, family relationships, broken relationships, casual relationships, and friendships. It is what Jesus clearly spelled out when He said, "I appointed you to go and produce lasting fruit" (John 15:16, Page 824).

Again, and again the Bible teaches about the importance of bearing fruit. But exactly how can we be fruitful? For the woman at the well, and for many new Christians, their excitement and zeal is so contagious, their transformation so obvious, that the Good News spills from them without hesitation. Authentic enthusiasm persuades others to explore and follow suit. But after the new wears off, often so does the infectious enthusiasm. A few rebuffs from people we care about, and we become a bit more cautious in sharing about what we've found in Jesus Christ. But that doesn't have to be, and should not be, the case.

Read the following verses:

Jeremiah 17:7-8 (Page 587)

Psalm 1:2-3 (Page 415)

List the characteristics of the Christ-followers described in these verses.

Did you notice it? They practice everything we've talked about in this study for finding purpose in every season and circumstance. They serve as ambassadors for Christ. They trust in God and have made Him their hope and confidence – not their own abilities, talents, or wealth. God's Word remains always on their minds – the natural result of consistently reading and meditating on it.

What is the analogy both passages use to describe someone whose trust is in God?

Trees – the type whose leaves always stay green no matter how shallow the water gets, no matter how hot the weather gets. *Nothing* causes them to wither so that even in the very worst of times they never stop producing fruit! Do you see the significance of these words? When we set our minds on God, when we fill our hearts with His Word, *no circumstance can cause us to wither.* Through every season, our steady confidence in God will grow our influence as we serve Him. We will always produce fruit.

> Read Matthew 13:23 (Page 744).

Wow! Thirty, sixty, or even *a hundred times* as much as had been invested! Sometimes we are aware of the fruit we produce but often we're not. The numbers aren't up to us. That's God's responsibility. Our responsibility is to faithfully and consistently live our lives by the standards God commands us. When we do that, our lives produce fruit.

> More than 700 people gathered in Liverpool, United Kingdom, for the first night of several evangelistic meetings. During the worship time, the speaker noticed a woman in the crowd whose glowing face caused her to stand out from those around her. When the singing concluded, and the speaker stepped to the podium, he invited her to share a word with everyone. Without hesitation, she stood and told about a random encounter she'd had eight years earlier with an old man in old clothes in downtown Sydney, Australia. "He asked me if I knew what would happen to me when I died," she said. "His question haunted me until I finally went to a church near my house and asked the pastor about it. At his encouragement, I started reading my Bible and learned about Jesus who'd died for me. I soon asked Him to forgive my sins and be my Lord and Savior. From that day on I've never doubted what will happen when I die."

> The next night, a similar thing happened. The speaker asked another random person in the audience to share something. This time it was a young military man who'd been stationed in Australia and who had a similar encounter with an old man in old clothes in downtown Sydney – with the exact same results.

CHAPTER 6 // BEAR FRUIT

On the third night, when the speaker again picked a random person from the crowd who shared about a similar encounter, he decided it was time to visit Sidney for himself. Upon arrival, he headed straight downtown and started walking up and down the streets. Before too many days passed, he ran into an old man in old clothes who approached him with a question. The man's name was Mr. Jenner. As he listened to the speaker's story, tears started to course down Mr. Jenner's cheeks. "Ten years ago," he said, "I promised God I would witness to at least one person every day. I never got discouraged, but this is the first time I knew I was making a difference."[7]

When we hold faithful to our God-given purpose, our lives bear fruit – everlasting fruit we may never know of until we step foot in Heaven. Bearing fruit is our most important significance on Earth because it makes an eternal difference. Anything we accomplish here on Earth, outside of this one, will fade away in time. The fruit we bear for Christ lasts forever.

As Jesus' time on Earth drew to a close, He prepared the disciples to carry out this most important of all assignments. He wanted them (and us) to know how to succeed in this mission and that they would not rely on their own strength. The Holy Spirit within them would guide them.

What is the key message of John 15:3-5 (Page 824)?

Stay connected to God! It's that simple. Remain in Him and you will bear fruit. You cannot bear fruit on your own; only God-in-you produces fruit.

Now read John 15:8-17 (Page 824).

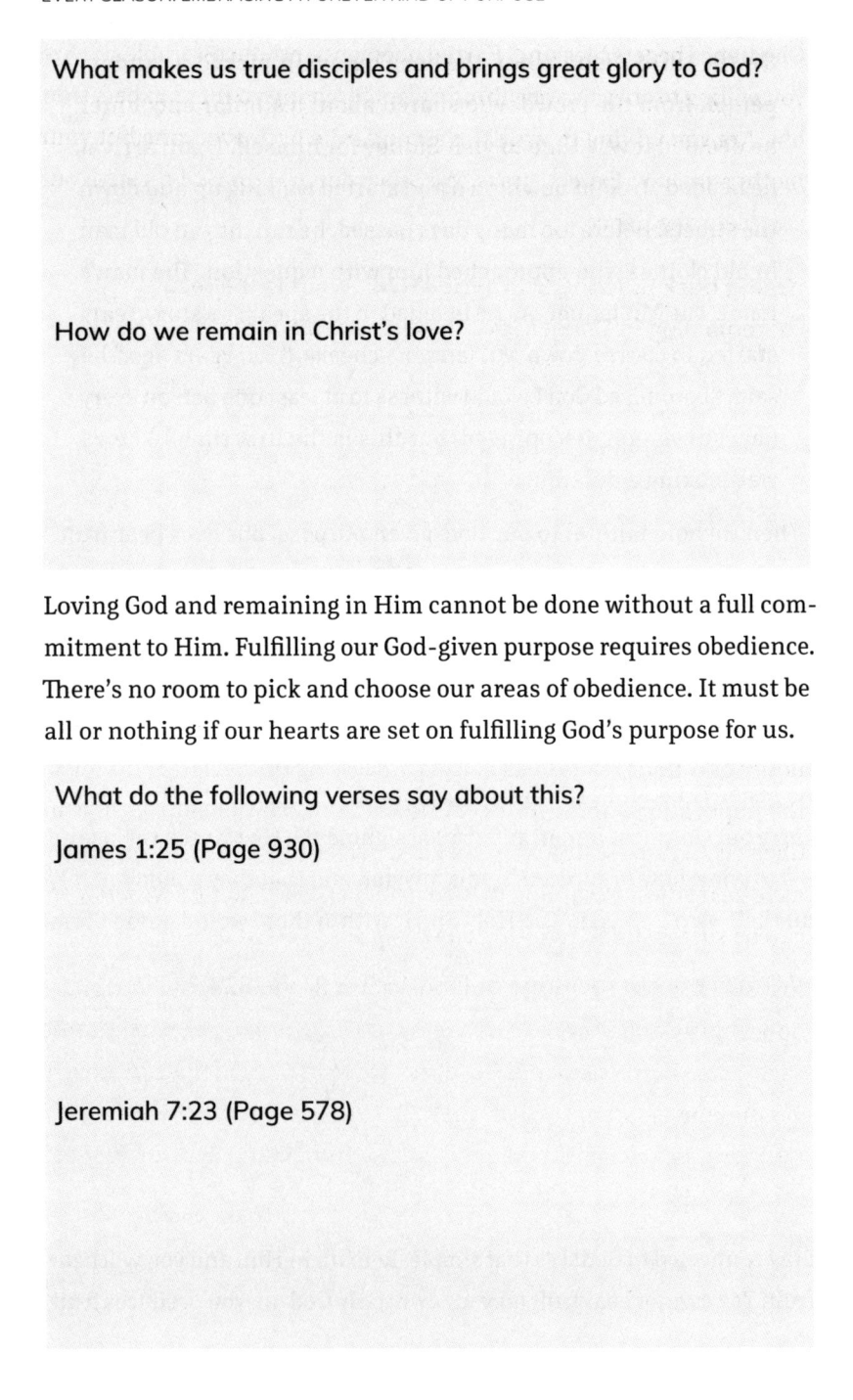

What makes us true disciples and brings great glory to God?

How do we remain in Christ's love?

Loving God and remaining in Him cannot be done without a full commitment to Him. Fulfilling our God-given purpose requires obedience. There's no room to pick and choose our areas of obedience. It must be all or nothing if our hearts are set on fulfilling God's purpose for us.

What do the following verses say about this?

James 1:25 (Page 930)

Jeremiah 7:23 (Page 578)

Obedience begets blessing. Partial obedience produces problems. Are you willing to obey in everything except forgiving your ex? Expect trouble. Are you willing to walk the second mile with everyone but your mother-in-law? Expect stress. We prove our love for God through our complete obedience.

> Going back to John 15:11 (Page 824), what is the result of remaining in Christ's love through obedience?

Not just filled with joy but *overflowing* with joy! God's joy will radiate through every season of our lives, the bright ones and the dark ones. His joy will fill us with a profound sense of eternal purpose – that includes bearing fruit because we are beloved by Christ. And, did you notice how Jesus refers to us in this passage? As His *friends!* Think about the implications of the level of intimacy! Our relationship with Jesus Christ is the most astonishing of gifts. Because of it, He has appointed us to be fruitful. According to John 15:16 (Page 824) how do we know we can be successful in fulfilling our purpose?

Just ask! Are you hesitant to talk about God to others? Just ask Him for opportunity and boldness. *He'll give it to you.* Are you not sure what to say? Just ask Him for words. *He'll provide them.* Are you not sure how to get the conversation started? Just ask Him for opportunity. *He'll make it happen.* Whatever it is that keeps you from being fruitful, just ask God for help. He will give you everything you need!

Reflect and Share

Is God prompting you to do something that you haven't yet done? Ask God to help you and share with your group so they can join you in prayer about this.

Closing Prayer

Father, I ask that You give me complete knowledge of Your will and spiritual wisdom and understanding so that the way I live will always honor and please You. Let my life produce every kind of good fruit. In all of this, let me grow as I learn to know You better and better. Strengthen me with all Your glorious power so I will have the endurance and patience I need. Fill me with joy, so that I am always thanking You because You have enabled me to share in the inheritance that belongs to Your people, who live in the light. Thank You for rescuing me from the kingdom of darkness and transferring me into the Kingdom of Your dear Son, who purchased my freedom and forgave my sins. Thank You for reconciling me to You through the death of Christ in His physical body. Thank You that this has brought me into Your presence where I stand holy and blameless before You without a single fault. Let me continue to believe this truth and stand firmly in it, not drifting away from the assurance I received when I heard the Good News. Amen. (Colossians 1:9-14, 22- 23, Page 902)

Would you like help in sharing your faith? Stonecroft offers a variety of resources to support and encourage you in this. See Page 115.

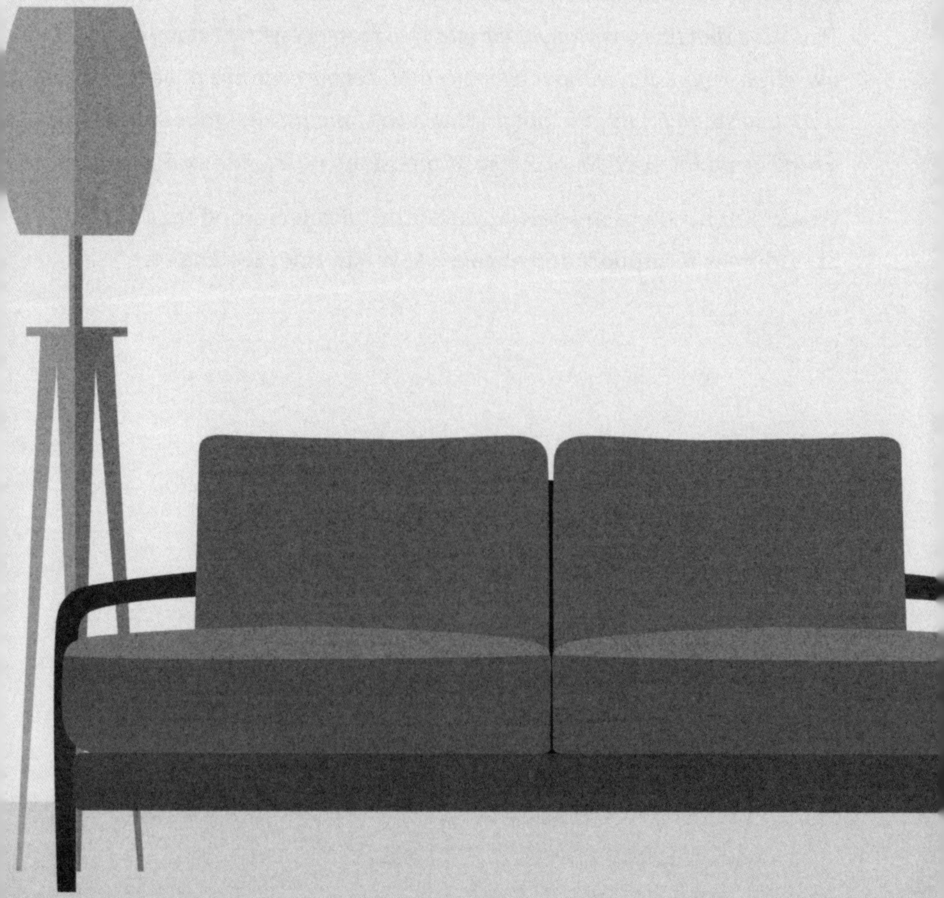

conclusion

Final Thoughts

Throughout the seasons of your life, your self-ordained plans will vary as your circumstances change and priorities and desires shift. Through these fluctuations, however, your God-given purpose remains unchanged. His purpose can, and should, buttress every purpose that drives you. God's purposes are eternal: *in every season, in every circumstance, be God's ambassador in your corner of the world.* This will bring Him glory.

Sometimes that corner will feel excruciatingly small – a hospital room, a jail cell, or physical or emotional limitations. Sometimes your corner will feel too large to manage – an opportunity that feels bigger than you, or a complex, unwieldy situation. Wherever you find yourself, you will always be accompanied with an opportunity to fulfill God's purpose. You will always, also be equipped with everything you need to achieve that purpose. God assures you of that.

Matthew 11:29-30 (MSG) reads, "Walk with me and work with me – watch how I do it. Learn the unforced rhythms of grace. I won't lay anything heavy or ill-fitting on you. Keep company with me and you'll learn to live freely and lightly." As you "keep company" with God throughout life, He cushions each season with His unexplainable peace as you learn His "unforced rhythms of grace." You are painting a living portrait that exquisitely portrays the value of a personal relationship with Jesus Christ. You may be the only ambassador of God some people meet. Your role then, as His image-bearer, is to be an enticing display of God-in-you, working in you, equipping and enabling you to be salt and light in all circumstances. This gives God the glory He desires. It's the one purpose that never changes and never becomes less important. In the end, it's the only one that matters.

In the introduction to this study, I described one hectic day with my preschool children as I tried to clean the house. God's light within me grew pretty dim. The good news is the story didn't end with my carpet ruined – or my faith crumbled. God used the events of that frustrating day to teach me a little more of His "unforced rhythms of grace," helping me to live freely and lightly even in that hectic season of life.

After finding the ink stain on my carpet I called every cleaning company in town looking for a solution to fix it. Their unanimous advice: *Put a rug over it.*

I just couldn't accept this, though. I had to try something. Getting a basin of water, a bar of soap, and a rag, I knelt by the stain and set to work, soaking up the ink, rinsing out the cloth, tears mingling with prayers as I worked. Soon, two pairs of chubby hands were patting my back. "We're sorry, Mommy!" they cried. Tyler ran for another cloth while Landon grabbed at the soap. The three of us circled the stain on our knees, soaking and rinsing and praying. Soaking and rinsing and praying. To my disbelieving eyes, the stain started to fade. It grew fainter and fainter, then disappeared. Completely. Not even a hint of discoloration. Truly a little miracle, if miracles can be little.

I sat back on my heels and stared in awe at my stain-free carpet, overwhelmed by God's love flooding that tiny bedroom – a less-than-microscopic piece of the entire universe. *Why would God care about my ink-stained carpet?* The thing is, He probably doesn't. But He does care about Landon, Tyler, and me. He is the expert when it comes to stain removal. There is no stain He can't make disappear. I kept proof of this for years, tucked in with my cleaning supplies. It was the cloth I used to soak up the ink. Despite countless washings, the cloth itself remained stained.

> *" ... as an image-bearer with a job to do, there is potential to reveal the glory of God in every circumstance, no matter how I feel, who I'm with, what my hands hold, or what's gone wrong. God with us lives within us. And he will come out through us in a million little ways."*[8]
>
> – Emily P. Freeman

Whatever stains mar your life, whatever stains kept you from reaching your potential or thwarted your dreams, God can remove them completely. His love for you covers every imaginable stain. Jesus, whose life on earth was perfect and stain-free, willingly died to remove your stains. Before God even laid the foundations of this incredible universe, He laid out His specific plan for your life. This is how the Bible explains it:

> "God decided in advance to adopt us into his own family by bringing us to himself through Jesus Christ. This is what he wanted to do, and it gave him great pleasure. So, we praise God for the glorious grace he has poured out on us who belong to his dear Son. He is so rich in kindness and grace that he purchased our freedom with the blood of his Son and forgave our sins. He has showered his kindness on us, along with all wisdom and understanding. God has now revealed to us his mysterious will regarding Christ – which is to fulfill his own good pleasure. And this is the plan: At the right time, he will bring everything together under the authority of Christ – everything in heaven and on earth. Furthermore, because we are united with Christ, we have received an inheritance from God, for he chose us in advance, and he makes everything work out according to his plan.
>
> "God's purpose was that we Jews who were the first to trust in Christ would bring praise and glory to God."
>
> – Ephesians 1:5-12 (Page 895)

Who we are. What we are living for. Our purpose in Christ: is to glorify God, worshipping Him as we are salt and light to the world around us, trusting Him, being His image-bearer, His ambassador, and always, always bearing fruit.

Those years when the boys were young felt too narrow to develop what I felt was my purpose. That time eventually passed. New seasons rushed in, broader ones offering more opportunity to use God's gifts and follow my passion. But time kept moving and now my accumulating years appear to narrow again as opportunities lessen and family needs increase. *But it is only the appearance of narrowing!* The reality to keep at the forefront of our minds is that our current season is exactly the size God wants it to be. Regardless of how purposeless our days may seem at any given time, in God's eyes our purpose is only growing more crucial.

Glorify Him – every day, in every way, until you draw your last earthly breath. *Then get ready.* The very next breath will fill your lungs with heavenly air and what comes next will exceed anything you've ever dared imagine. *And it will be worth it all.*

> Review your Reflect and Share sections of each chapter. Then, spend some time praying together.
>
> What have you learned in this season?

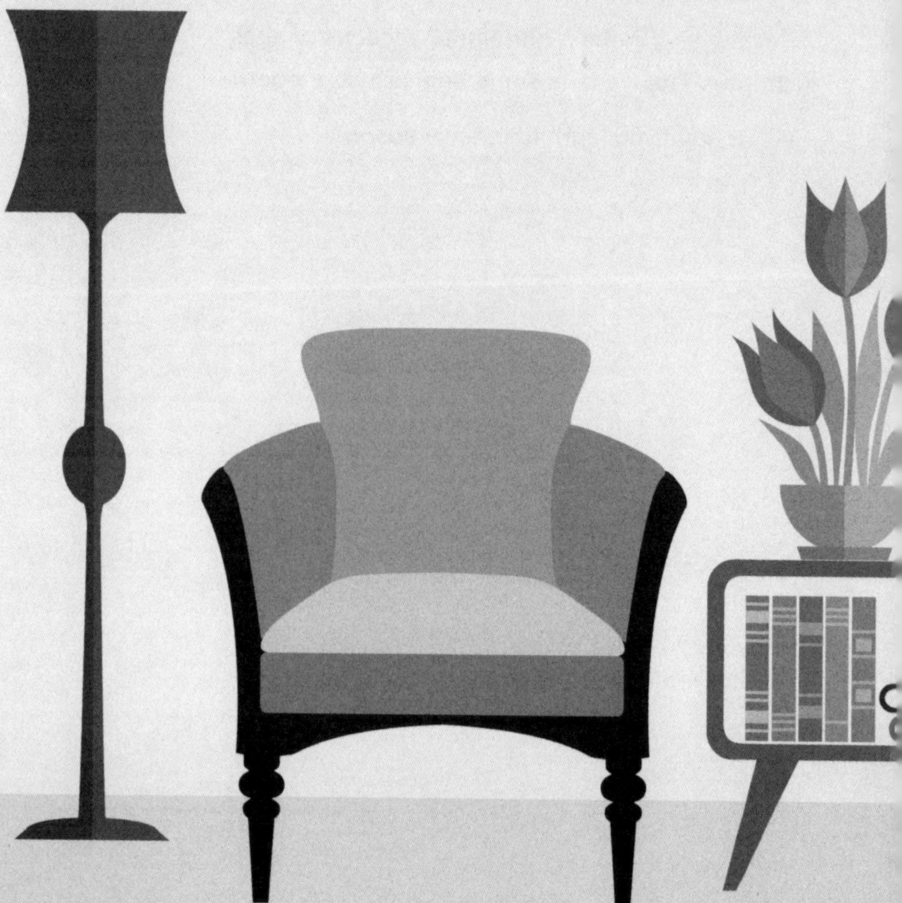

God's Pursuing Love

God, who created the universe, is full of love and mercy. He desires for you to personally receive His love and mercy.

It doesn't matter what has happened in your past. No matter what you've done, no matter what's been done to you, no matter what you regret about how you've lived your life, God's mercy is greater. God understands you – your hopes, your dreams, your frustrations, your loneliness, your heartaches. His love caused Him to pursue us, to leave heaven and come to Earth.

"For God so loved the world that he gave his one and only Son, that whoever believes in him shall not perish but have eternal life. For God did not send his Son into the world to condemn the world, but to save the world through him."

– John 3:16-17, NIV

God is love. He is a God of relationship.

God created us to have a real and personal relationship with Him. Sin keeps us from having a loving relationship with God. We all have sinned and been separated from God. We all carry sin's consequences in our lives.

But God the Father loves so deeply that He made a way to close the gap of separation. He sent His Son, Jesus, to Earth to live a perfect life with no sin and then to die in our place. Jesus Christ took the punishment for our sin. Jesus is God and He did the work for us.

Nothing we can do will earn us God's love. No good works. No good deeds. No avoidance of evil. "For God made Christ, who never sinned, to be the offering for our sin, so that we could be made right with God through Christ" (2 Corinthians 5:21, NIV).

"But God is so rich in mercy, and he loved us so much, that even though we were dead because of our sins, he gave us life when he raised Christ from the dead. (It is only by God's grace that you have been saved!)"

– Ephesians 2:4-5 (Page 895)

Jesus Christ paid the penalty for sin when He died on the cross. But He did not stay dead! He came back to life, He rose from the dead. And He is ready to share His life with you.

Jesus is alive today. He offers reconciliation to us. He can give you a new beginning and a newly created life. "This means that anyone who belongs in Christ has become a new person. The old life is gone; a new life has begun!" (2 Corinthians 5:17, Page 884).

How do you begin this new life? Place your trust in Jesus Christ. Believe that He is God and receive His love. Agree with God about your sin and believe that Jesus came to close the separation between you and God. Ask Jesus to lead your life.

When you trust Jesus Christ, He will live in your life. God's Spirit will live inside you. This Holy Spirit will help you live a life that honors Him.

Do you want to begin this new life? You can start today with a few simple words like, "Dear Jesus, I believe that You are God and that You love me and came to save me through Your death and resurrection."

Or you might pray something like this:

Jesus, I believe You are the Son of God and that You died on the cross to pay the penalty for my sin. Forgive me. I choose to turn away from my sin and live a life that honors You. I want to follow You and make You the leader of my life. Thank You for Your gift of eternal life and for the Holy Spirit who now has come to live in me. Amen.

Stonecroft wants to offer you a free publication called *A New Beginning.* This short Bible study will help you get started on your new faith journey. You can order a free copy by filling out the form found on the lower part of this webpage: stonecroft.org/know-god. The form includes a small box to check to request a downloadable copy of *A New Beginning.* You will want a Bible. We recommend the New Living Translation (NLT).

May God move mightily in response to your prayers!

Notes

INTRODUCTION

1. Emily P. Freeman, Part 1 {"Who is the Artist?"} & Chapter 1 {Awake} – Fall 2013 Bloom – *A Million Little Ways,* Emily P. Freeman, http://emilypfreeman.com/million-little-ways-book-club-videos/ (site accessed January 2017).

CHAPTER TWO

2. Emily P. Freeman, *A Million Little Ways* (Grand Rapids: Revell, 2013), 189.

CHAPTER THREE

3. Franklin Graham. *Living Beyond the Limits* (Nashville: Thomas Nelson, 1998), 33-53.

CHAPTER FOUR

4. John Kavanaugh, S.J. "Clarity vs. Trust." *America*, July 29, 1995, 38.

5. Rick Warren, "Living A Life of Service." Pastor Rick's Daily Hope (blog), May 21, 2014. Accessed May, 2017. http://rickwarren.org/devotional/english/living-a-life-of-service_273

6. Freeman, *A Million Little Ways*, 40.

CHAPTER SIX

7. Alice Gray, "The Sower," in *Stories for a Faithful Heart*, compiled by Alice Gray (Sisters: Multnomah Press, 2000), 75-76.

8. Freeman, *A Million Little Ways*, 191.

Works Cited

Graham, Franklin. *Living Beyond the Limits*. Nashville, TN: Thomas Nelson, 1998.

Freeman, Emily P. "Part 1: Who Is the Artist?" and "Chapter 1: Awake" Emily P. Freeman. October 17, 2013. Accessed January 2017. http://emilypfreeman.com/million-little-ways-book-club-videos/.

Freeman, Emily P. *A Million Little Ways*. Grand Rapids, MI: Revell, 2013.

Gray, Alice. "The Sower." In *Stories for a Faithful Heart*, 75-76. Sisters, OR: Multnomah Press, 2000.

Kavanaugh, John S.J. *America*, July 29, 1995.

Warren, Rick. "Living a Life of Service." Pastor Rick's Daily Hope (blog), May 21, 2014. Accessed May 2017. http://rickwarren.org/devotional/english/living-a-life-of-service_273.

Who is Stonecroft?

Every day Stonecroft communicates the Gospel in meaningful ways. Whether side-by-side with a neighbor or new friend, or through a speaker sharing her transformational story, the Gospel of Jesus Christ goes forward. Through a variety of outreach activities and small-group Bible studies specifically designed for those not familiar with God, and with online and print resources focused on evangelism, Stonecroft proclaims the love of Jesus Christ to women where they are, as they are.

For more than 80 years, Stonecroft volunteers have found ways to introduce women to Jesus Christ and train them to share His Good News with others – always with a foundation of prayer and reliance on God.

Stonecroft understands and appreciates the influence of one woman's life. When you reach her, you touch everyone she knows – her family, friends, neighbors, and co-workers. The real truth of the Gospel brings real redemption into real lives.

Our life-changing, faith-building community resources include:

- Stonecroft Bible Studies

   We offer both topical and chapter-by-chapter studies. We designed Stonecroft studies for those in small groups to simply, yet profoundly, discover God's Word together.

- *Conversations*

   These thought-provoking small-group resources engage women in conversation on topics that matter. *Conversations* include *Rest*, *Known*, and *Enough*.

- Stonecroft Prays

   This tool helps small groups of women pray for God to show them avenues to reach women in their community with the Gospel.

- Outreach Events

    These set the stage for women to hear and share the Gospel with their communities. Whether in a large venue, workshop, or small group setting, Stonecroft women find ways to share the love of Christ.

- Stonecroft Military

    This specialized effort honors women connected to the U.S. military and shares with them the Gospel while showing them the love of Christ.

- Stonecroft Aware Series

    These resources reveal God's heart for those who do not yet know Him. The Aware Series includes *Aware*, *Belong*, and *Call*.

- stonecroft.org

    Our site offers fresh content daily to equip and encourage you.

Dedicated and enthusiastic Stonecroft staff and volunteers serve together to engage women in sharing the love of Christ with the world. Your life matters. Join us today to become part of reaching your communities with the Gospel of Jesus Christ. Become involved with Stonecroft.

For more information, contact:

Stonecroft

connections@stonecroft.org

800.525.8627

stonecroft.org

Resources

Ephesians
Reflect on the big love of God and find His strength and power to live victoriously.
7 chapters

Loving Your Neighbors
Seek God's heart and compassion for your neighbors through this prayer resource.
12 chapters

Prayer Worth Repeating
This small-group resource offers biblical insights and helps you pray together for your adult children.
15 chapters

Living in God's Will
Each chapter of this study of Ruth works to build your freedom and confidence in God's guidance.
7 chapters

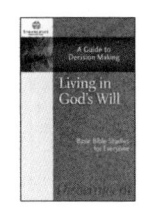

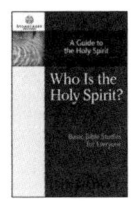

Who is the Holy Spirit?
Consider who the Holy Spirit is. Become more aware of God's activity in your life.
6 chapters

About the Author

Janice Mayo Mathers is the author of several books, including *Loving Your Neighbors* and *Ephesians: Made Complete in Christ*, both recently published by Stonecroft. She has been a columnist with *Today's Christian Woman* and *Virtue* magazines. A conference and retreat speaker, Janice also serves as a member of the National Board of Directors and as a Speaker Consultant for Stonecroft. She lives in Bend, Oregon, where she and her husband, Steve, operate a four-generation well-drilling business

Stonecroft
where she is ✣ as she is